The Church:
The Gifted and
The Retarded Child

The Church:
The Gifted and
The Retarded Child

By
Charles F. Kemp

 THE BETHANY PRESS
ST. LOUIS, MO.

To

Mr. and Mrs. Frank Hurley

Contents

Introduction

".... to one he gave five talents, to another two, to another one, to each according to his ability."—Matthew 25:15. If this study needs a text, this is it. Jesus recognized the truth of individual differences centuries ago.

What Do We Mean by Individual Differences?

No two people are exactly alike. Every baby born in the hospital is different from every other baby. Every school day in America more than 30,000,000 children and young people leave their homes and go to school. No two of them are the same. Every child is different from every other child. Every man in the street, every man in the factory, every person in the home, everyone in a congregation is different from everyone else. Even identical twins have their differences. All people are different. They are different in appearance, in height, in weight; they differ in physical strength, in the speed with which they can run, in their ability to sing, in their ability to master certain skills, in their ability to understand, to solve problems, to think. In some of these areas the degree of difference is quite marked.

In this study we are interested primarily in intelligence. It is common knowledge that people differ very greatly in their mental powers or intellectual abilities. We quote the statement, "All men are created equal," which in one sense is true, or should be. Men should be equal in their claim to freedom, equal in their rights before the law, equal in their right to learn; but men are not equal in capacity, they are not equal in ability. "To one he gave five talents, to another two, to another one, to each *according to his ability.*" At one extreme are those rare souls who have great talent, those geniuses who stand head and shoulders above the rest. They have ability to understand, to create, to invent, to lead. At the other end of the scale are those few who cannot master even the simplest skills; they cannot solve the simplest problems; their understanding is and always will be very limited.

For centuries men have puzzled over this fact. Why people differ so greatly in their ability to learn has been one of the mysteries of the ages. Only recently are we beginning to understand some of the facts about man and his intelligence. For some time now it has been a concern of the public school. In every school, in almost every classroom, there is a wide range of abilities among the pupils. As we shall stress later, this is true also in every Sunday church school and in every congregation. Psychologists have been studying intelligence for many years. It has been the subject of as much research and investigation as any area of human nature. We have an understanding of man and his mental abilities today that we have not had before.

What Is Intelligence?

With all this investigation we do not actually know what intelligence is. We really cannot define it. We cannot see it. We cannot feel it. We cannot touch it. We cannot examine it. We cannot study it under a microscope or measure it with a yardstick. We cannot weigh it on the most delicate scales. Yet we speak of people as being intelligent, and everyone knows what we mean. We can observe it in action. In essence that is what intelligence tests do: they observe certain actions and then compare the results with the actions of many other people. Intelligence consists of many things—planning, judging, remembering, solving problems, learning, profiting from past experience, or just being able to get along in this complicated world. All of this requires intelligence.

How Is Intelligence Measured?

Men have always wondered how intelligence can be determined, how we can tell how much intelligence a person has. We cannot tell by appearance, although we all do judge others by how they look. This is evidenced by such common expressions as, "He is an intelligent-looking man," or "He looks like a dull child." No one would claim that this is any real measure of intelligence. Dr. Harry J. Baker points out that some very good-looking individuals are in homes for the feeble-minded and some of our greatest geniuses appear very ordinary, even inadequate.[1]

Among school children grades are a good clue, although at times they are inaccurate. In this volume we shall cite examples of pupils, who, for some reason or other, received poor grades but who, when a careful examination was made, were found to have good minds, in some cases brilliant minds. Of course, the opposite is also true sometimes. When such a situation occurs, there are always other factors present, either in the experience of the pupil or the teacher, but they serve to remind us that teachers are fallible and

[1] Cf. H. J. Baker, *Introduction to Exceptional Children*, Macmillan, 1947, p. 224.

school grades are very subjective in nature and open to human error.

In order to meet this problem psychologists and educators devised what is known as "the intelligence test." It has had a long and interesting history, too long to review here except to mention some of the names that have been most prominently associated with the testing movement. Sir Francis Galton, of England, was very much interested in individual differences, especially as they related to genius. He did much to stimulate the thought of others, and some people feel that he should be considered the originator of the idea. James McKeen Cattell was the first to use the term "mental tests," and is usually considered the father of the testing movement in America. Alfred Binet, of France, made perhaps the greatest single contribution. We shall speak more of him and his work later. There were many others: T. H. Simon, who collaborated with Binet; Edward Thorndike, at Columbia University, who made the oft-quoted statement, "Whatever exists at all exists in some amount and therefore can be measured"; Arthur S. Otis, whose work was taken over by the Army to become the Army Alpha Test; and Lewis M. Terman, of Stanford University, who adapted the Binet scale for use in this country.

There were many others, thousands in fact, for tests have been used very widely in education, in the army, in industry, and in other areas. The result is that the whole field has been greatly developed. We now have group tests and individual tests, performance tests designed for those who have a language handicap, specialized tests for those who have a visual, an auditory, or some other physical handicap or limitation.

We cannot discuss it further here except to say that the

intelligence test correctly administered is without doubt the best single measure of intellectual ability that we have today. A good test is completely impartial and unprejudiced. It is standardized on thousands of subjects and thus it enables us to compare an individual not merely with others in his local group but with a cross section of the whole population. It should be added that the test must be a good one and must be administered in the proper way. There are literally hundreds of tests, to say nothing of quizzes that appear in popular magazines, and one should not base a judgment on anything but a standard test. It should be recognized that an individual test is more reliable than a group test and that persons with a language difficulty or some limitation in sight or hearing should have a test designed for their use. It should also be recognized that tests can be in error. The tester may give the test poorly, the individual may not be feeling well or may not be motivated to make his best effort. If test results give an indication of ability that is different from that which the person's classroom and other behavior might indicate, he should be retested. Even the test specialists warn that tests are only clues as to what exists. When the experts issue such warnings, the laymen should be cautious; nevertheless, tests still give the best single indication of intelligence that we have. For that reason we shall refer to intelligence tests and intelligence test scores frequently in this volume. We do not mean to imply that the pastor or religious educator should be a specialist in testing or that he should attempt to administer tests. Quite to the contrary, we feel that this should be left to those who are trained and qualified to do so. We do feel that the pastor and religious educator should have an understanding of what the tests mean, what the scores actually indicate, for they can have a direct and definite bearing upon their work, both with individuals and in the program of the church as a whole.

There are two measures that we should mention for we will probably refer to them many times. They are the "mental age" or MA and the "intelligence quotient" or the familiar IQ. The mental age as a concept was first introduced by Binet. It indicates a level of mental development. Thus a bright child of chronological age (CA) of ten years may have a mental age of twelve, or even fifteen, years. A dull child of chronological age of ten years may have an MA of nine or eight years. Both may be in the same classroom. The intelligence quotient, or IQ, is a measure of brightness, or of comparative mental ability. It is found by dividing the mental age by the chronological age and multiplying by 100. ($100\dfrac{MA}{CA} = IQ$). In other words, this is a measure of brightness that shows how the child's mental age compares with his chronological age and it gives a comparative measure, whatever his chronological age may be.

How Is Intelligence Distributed?

One of the most interesting phenomena about intelligence is the uniform way in which it is distributed throughout the general population, with approximately the same number at one end of the scale as at the other, and also with a proportionate distribution throughout. It is much easier to illustrate than to describe. Fig. 1, shows what is known as the normal curve of distribution and appears in almost every beginning text in psychology or education.

Of course, intelligence is not the only thing that follows the normal curve. The distribution of height, weight, strength and handgrip, the ability to read, even the height of stalks of corn in a cornfield or the size of pumpkins in a garden all follow the normal curve of distribution. This sounds like an exaggeration but there is ample research to prove it.[2]

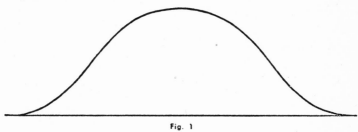

Fig. 1

Applying the curve to the distribution of intelligence in terms of IQ's we find the following facts as they are pictured in Fig. 2.

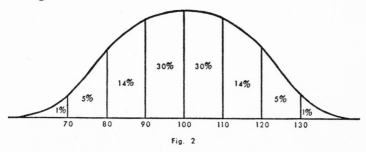

Fig. 2

100 is the mid-point of the distribution. Approximately 30 per cent of the population will measure from 100 to 110; 14 per cent from 110 to 119; 5 per cent from 120 to 129, and 1 per cent will be 130 and above. Moving left from

2 Cf. W. D. Commins, *Principles of Educational Psychology*, The Ronald Press, 1937, pp. 55-58.

the mid-point, the same percentages will prevail.[3] The psychologists whose research reveals these results have assigned certain names to sections of the distribution, such as idiot, imbecile, moron, borderline, average, superior, and genius. It should be pointed out that some of these are technical terms and should not be used by the layman unless he is familiar with their meanings.

Education has made a great deal of use of these facts. Fig. 3 is an illustration of the way in which the normal

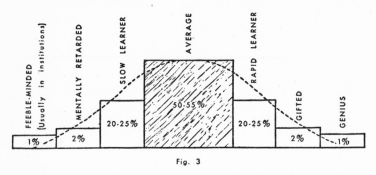

Fig. 3

curve has been utilized for educational purposes. Actually it would be a curve like the dotted line, but we have put it in blocks for purposes of clarification. You will note also that the names assigned to the groups have an educational connotation,[4] which is accepted in a standard text on the education of exceptional children. It is recognized, as he points out, that percentages are approximate and there are actually no clear-cut lines between the groups.

This figure presenting the picture from the educator's point of view has much to suggest to the church and to religious education. For our purposes in this study we can

[3] Cf. *Ibid.*, p. 180.
[4] The names and percentages are taken from Baker, *op. cit.*, p. 239.

go one step farther and simplify it a bit more. For all practical purposes the two small blocks to the extreme right in Fig. 3 can be combined into one and called "the gifted." Also, the two small blocks to the left can be combined into one and called "the retarded." In both cases their degree of divergence from the average is so large and their percentage is so small that they can be considered together. We are not concerned only with the 3 per cent who are extremely gifted but with all who are above average; nor are we concerned only with the extremely retarded but with the problems of all who are below average. Since our interest is not only in learning but in the total life adjustment, we will use the terms "above" and "below average," rather than rapid and slow learners. Revising our chart once again it would appear like this.

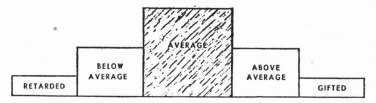

Fig. 4

Many studies have already dealt with the religious education and guidance of the average. In our study here we are interested primarily in those children and young people in our churches who fall in the two blocks to the right and the two to the left of the "average" or shaded areas in Fig. 4. In other words, we are dealing with those who have great intellectual potential on one hand, and those who have an intellectual handicap or limitation on the other.

There is much difference of opinion as to whether intelligence is general or specific. Thorndike, for example, felt it was general. Thurstone, on the other hand, feels it is composed of many factors, each quite separate from the other. It is quite generally recognized that two people may have the same intelligence quotient but they may differ in the things they can do well. For this reason, Thurstone feels there are different kinds of intelligence which he calls "primary mental abilities." He listed seven, although he did not consider this final. These are verbal meaning or comprehension, space perception, number ability, word fluency, reasoning ability, memory, and perception. Some of the new intelligence tests take these factors into account, giving a verbal IQ, etc. Whether intelligence is conceived as some general (g) factor or whether it consists of a combination of mental abilities, it is highly important in the success and place one finds in life.

How Does This Affect the Church?

This whole subject of intelligence and individual differences has received much interest and attention in recent years. It has been a subject of great concern to several professions, especially educators, psychologists, and social workers. It has caught a great deal of popular attention and has been the subject of numerous articles in popular magazines. Thus far the church has been negligent at this point. The books on the psychology of religion have little to say about it. The pastoral psychology movement has said much about counseling but has had almost nothing to say about the gifted or the retarded and their problems. Even religious education has overlooked it to a large extent and has made no major emphasis on individual differences and has made little use of the research that has been done in this field.

Why should the church be concerned? In the first place, the church should be concerned because the church is concerned about everyone—rich and poor, old and young, wise and simple. It is the essence of the Christian message that all men are children of God, that everyone is of value in his sight. This is true whether the person is gifted or retarded.

Fig. 5—MENTAL AGES

Chrono-logical Age	Retarded Average I.Q. 67	Slow Learner Average I.Q. 83	Average Average I.Q. 100	Rapid Learner Average IQ. 117	Gifted Average I.Q. 133
1	8 mo.	10 mo.	1	1 yr. 2 mo.	1 yr. 4 mo.
2	1 yr. 4 mo.	1 yr. 8 mo.	2	2 yr. 4 mo.	2 yr. 8 mo.
3	2	2 yr 6 mo.	3	3 yr. 6 mo.	4 yr.
4	2 yr. 8 mo.	3 yr 4 mo.	4	4 yr. 8 mo.	5 yr. 4 mo.
5	3 yr. 4 mo.	4 yr. 2 mo	5	5 yr 10 mo.	6 yr. 8 mo.
6	4	5	6	7	8
7	4 yr. 8 mo.	5 yr. 10 mo.	7	8 yr. 2 mo.	9 yr. 4 mo.
8	5 yr. 4 mo	6 yr. 8 mo.	8	9 yr. 4 mo.	10 yr. 8 mo.
9	6	7 yr. 6 mo.	9	10 yr. 6 mo.	12
10	6 yr. 8 mo.	8 yr. 4 mo.	10	11 yr 8 mo.	13 yr. 4 mo.
11	7 yr. 4 mo.	9 yr. 2 mo.	11	12 yr. 10 mo.	14 yr. 8 mo.
12	8 .	10	12	14	16
13	8 yr. 8 mo	10 yr. 10 mo.	13	15 yr 2 mo	17 yr 4 mo.
14	9 yr. 4. mo.	11 yr. 8 mo.	14	16 yr 4 mo	18 yr. 8 mo.
15	10 yr.	12 yr. 6 mo.	15	17 yr. 6 mo.	20

The pastor will have both groups in his congregation. The normal curve of distribution applies to his congregation as well as to the population as a whole. Perhaps those to the extreme left or lower end of the scale will not be there, for they will be in institutions, and those geniuses to the extreme right may not be in every congregation; nevertheless, both the gifted and the retarded, the above average and the below average, the rapid learner and the slow learner sit side by side in every congregation. If his message is to have value to all, it must take this into account.

Both groups are present in the church school. This can present a real problem of instruction. See, for example, the chart in Fig. 5. The column to the left is chronological age. The other five columns are mental ages. When a child is one year old, if his IQ is 67 (the average for the retarded group), his mental age, as listed in the first column, will be eight months. If his IQ is 83 (the average for slow learners), his mental age will be ten months. If his IQ is 100, of course his MA and CA will be the same. If his IQ is 117 (the average for the rapid learners), his MA will be one year and 2 months. If his IQ is 133 (the average for the gifted), his MA will be one year and 4 months—a space of eight months' difference in one year.

Now drop down to six years of age when, in most school systems, children enter the first grade. Now the space is from an MA of 4 years for the retarded to 8 years for the gifted. Go on down to age 12, or about the beginning of junior high. Here the retarded youngster has an MA of 8 years, the slow learner 10, the rapid learner 14, and the gifted 16—yet all may be in the same church school class. At 15, or at the high school level, the range is from 10 to 20, but all may be in the same youth group.

All of these young people are important. Each one has his own problems and his own needs. From the very practical standpoint of instruction and planning programs of interest to all, the problem is obvious. It is even difficult to phrase routine questions that will be understood by all. More than this is the difficulty of meeting the needs of all.

S. R. Laycock states, "True democracy means attempting to give all children the best possible opportunity to develop to the limits of their own possibilities."[5] The National Society for the Study of Education says, "Inherent in the philosophy of democracy is the doctrine that every child is entitled to an education to the limit of his capacity."[6] These statements written about democracy and education apply equally to the church and its responsibility. Every child—both the gifted and the retarded—should have the best possible opportunity to develop to the limits of his own spiritual possibilities. Every child is entitled to a religious or a Christian education to the limits of his capacity and understanding. Many do not get it now.

The pastor or religious educator will not only have these people in his congregation and in his church school classes; he will often be expected to give them guidance as individuals. An understanding of their intellectual capacities could have a real bearing in such areas as marriage counseling and vocational choice, for instance. Let us take one example. Much is being said about church vocations these days and the need for recruitment. Here the pastor is expected to be a specialist. How can he give wise guidance to a young person considering the ministry if he does not know whether the person has the intellectual capacity to do college and seminary work?

We recognize that there are other factors besides intelligence that determine success in life. Achievement, whether it is in the vocational world, the home, or in personal development, depends on many things—on motivation, environmental opportunities, personality, char-

[5] Laycock, *Journal of Exceptional Children*, Feb. 1952, pp. 129-132.
[6] National Society for the Study of Education, *Education of Exceptional Children* (49th Yearbook, Part 2) University of Chicago Press, 1950, p. 3.

acter, as well as ability. It is a combination of all these factors and many more. Here we are dealing with intelligence as it relates to all of these other aspects of life. One of the problems the church must face is how this intelligence is to be used. How can it be motivated for the service of all?

What Is the Plan of This Book?

This study is divided into two main sections, one on the gifted and one on the retarded. We will follow the same general outline in both sections. In each there will be: (1) an introductory chapter that will attempt to point up the problem, show the nature and extent of the problem as it exists today. (2) a historical section. It is our opinion that we can understand the problem as we see it in perspective only when we understand what others have done. (3) a chapter on the psychology of both the gifted and the retarded. We need to understand the gifted and the retarded before we can help them. This will draw heavily on the research of psychologists and educators for they are the ones who have given this the most attention. (4) and (5) two chapters in which we will move directly into the program of the church, first dealing with the way these findings, as outlined in the first three chapters, apply to religious education, and then the way they apply to the field of guidance as carried on by the pastor or religious educator.

Although the outlines are the same, there will be obvious differences of treatment. In discussing religious education of the retarded we must consider religious education as it affects those in institutions for the retarded. This does not apply in the case of the gifted. In discussing guidance the nondirective or client-centered approach has a much more direct bearing on the guidance of the gifted than it does on the guidance of the retarded, for, while the basic attitudes of acceptance, both of the limitations and feelings still apply, the retarded cannot be expected to enter into the relationship in the same manner.

Let it be pointed out that this is an introduction. It is a new field. There is practically no research from the standpoint of the church from which to draw. It is hoped that this study will stimulate others to give it much thought and that many will go far beyond anything that is found here.

We express our indebtedness to many people who have contributed to this volume. Almost everything comes from some source, some book or some journal. We have attempted to give credit for all direct quotations but we would like to express general appreciation to all who contributed to this study, especially to Dr. Dean A. Worcester, formerly head of the Department of Educational Psychology at the University of Nebraska, who, more than any other, has given us an understanding of this problem.

Part I

The Gifted

Every one to whom much is given,
of him will much be required. . . . .

—*Luke 12:48b*

Chapter I

Our Wasted Talents:
The Nature and Extent of the Problem

There is a common misconception that to speak of the gifted, or those above average, is to speak of some group apart, some isolated few who are quite different from the rest of us. This is not true. To speak of the gifted is not to be talking about a separate group. The gifted are present in every community. There is the possibility of having one of great potential ability in any school, in any church, in any youth group. As to how many there are, no one really knows. Various figures have been suggested. There are more than 30,000,000 school children in the United States. If we take the top 20-25 per cent as above average, that gives us an army of more than 7,500,000 children of above average ability. If we take just the top 3 per cent, those above 130 IQ, those usually considered quite gifted, we have more than 900,000. If we limit it to the top 1 per cent, the very top of the scale, we still have more than 300,000. This is a sizable number.

The percentages mentioned above are based on national figures and may not apply in every community. A university town of 10,000 people, in which the faculty members and their families make up a large portion of the community, may have a higher percentage of intellectually gifted children than a factory town of 10,000 people. A congregation of 700 in the university town, in which faculty families comprise a large part of the congregation, will no doubt have a larger number of gifted children than a congregation of 700 in the factory town. This is nothing against the factory town, nor is it saying that one church is more important than the other. It is a recognition of the fact that intellectually gifted parents are likely to have intellectually gifted children.

The important thing to remember is that the gifted child may be found anywhere. Hodgenville, Kentucky, Diamond Grove, Missouri, Pottsgrove, Pennsylvania, would not be communities which we might expect to produce men of national prominence; yet in Hodgenville, Kentucky, Abraham Lincoln, the statesman, was born; near Diamond Grove, Missouri, George Washington Carver, the Negro scientist, was born; and in Pottsgrove, Pennsylvania, Washington Gladden, the religious leader, was born. We may be surprised at times. Even in the New Testament, when Nathanael was told about Jesus of Nazareth, he replied, "Can any thing good come out of Nazareth?"

We are not interested in percentages or even in total numbers as much as we are in the fact that there may be *one* gifted person in any community. From the standpoint of the pastor, the important thing is that there may be one in his town, in his church, in his youth group who has great potential, great possibilities for leadership and service.

The church should be concerned about these gifted young people for three reasons: first, because of the good they can do; second, because of the harm they can do; and third, because they are individuals and have their own needs and problems. All of these reasons are important. The very fact that they are gifted causes some difficulties. The problems of the delinquent, the handicapped, the underprivileged, and the retarded receive much attention. Problems of the gifted are often not even recognized. We shall discuss this at some length in the sections on the psychology and the guidance of the gifted. It must be recognized also that the gifted can do much harm. There have been many instances in history where brilliant minds have been devoted to unscrupulous ends with unfortunate results for all. A smart crook is more dangerous than a stupid one. When great intellect is misused for unethical, selfish, destructive, or harmful purposes, it is a social menace. The church, which is concerned about morals, ethics, social justice, law, the good of all, must be concerned that our most capable minds are directed into wholesome and constructive channels. The encouraging thing is the good that these people can do. No one can estimate the possibilities for good that lie within these gifted children and young people if they can be recognized, reached, and challenged.

Actually there is no clear-cut line between the gifted and the rest of the population. If we speak in terms of percentages, we usually refer to the top three per cent as gifted and the top 20-25 per cent as above average. If we speak in terms of IQ, the question of where giftedness begins or where the average leaves off is quite debatable. For example, if the dividing line is set at 130, where does the child with an IQ of 129 belong? On another test, on another day, he might score 131. The opposite might also be true. There is another factor that should be remembered. If one young person has an IQ of 109 and another of 111, one is considered average and the other above average; yet they are only two points apart. If one young person has an IQ of 109 and another an IQ of 91, they are both within the group listed as average, yet they are 18 points apart. Such thoughts should keep us from being too hasty in placing people within categories. Academically it is generally felt that an IQ of 110 or above is necessary for the college level and 125 or above for the Ph.D. level,[1] although there are some who would score below 110 who still secure college degrees by making extra effort. There are also some who score much higher who flunk out of school, but the reason is lack of motivation or some other complicating factor, and not lack of ability.

While speaking of IQ scores, we should point out that there are some areas of giftedness that do not appear on an IQ score at all. Intelligence tests do not reveal high artistic ability or social leadership. They do not show those who are above average in music, drawing, or dramatics. They do not reveal those who have the ability to get along with their fellows, or the ability to challenge and lead a group. Usually high talent in such areas also has a component in intelligence but it may not always show on an intelligence test. These are areas of achievement in which a person can be gifted or above average and all must be included if we use the terms aright.

Some people may prefer other terms than those we are using here. In the literature on the subject many terms are used interchangeably, such as superior, brilliant, talented, or genius. They all imply the capacity for outstanding achievement.

One of the tragedies of our gifted youth is that so few make the contribution of which they are capable. This is one point at which all who have studied this problem agree. The writings of such men and women as Lewis

[1] Cf. Passow, Goldberg, Tannenbaum, French, *Planning for Talented Youth*, Columbia University, 1955, p. 19.

Terman, Leta Hollingworth, Paul Witty, and Ruth Strang emphasize the great loss to society that is a result of our failure to recognize those who might have made, or might be making, great contributions. Several studies have been made that show that a large percentage of our most capable high school students do not go on to college. Going to college is no guarantee that an individual will make a contribution to the world, and the fact that a person does not go to college does not mean that he will not make a contribution—but it does mean that many who could have profited from further training do not receive it. A fact that all must realize is that many gifted people are making only a mediocre contribution to society, and some who could be contributing much are contributing nothing at all.

Here, for instance, is a young man in a Midwestern community, as reported by the University of Chicago Youth Development Program.[2] When he was ten years of age, he received an IQ score of 180 on the Cornell-Coxe Ability Scale. This score would be anticipated only once in a thousand times. It would indicate that this boy was as good as the average eighteen-year-old at the tasks that made up this test. In fact he scored so high that they thought there might be a mistake, so they retested him with another test and secured the same results. A series of other tests showed that he had a genius for visualizing objects in two or three dimensions, the kind of ability that would enable him to be a remarkable architect or construction engineer.

His father worked in a factory. Neither his father nor his mother had completed high school. They wanted him

[2] This illustration taken from the files of the University of Chicago Youth Development Program and reported by Robert J. Havighurst in the booklet, "Are the Community and the School Failing the Unusual Child?" University of Chicago Round Table, Number 735, April 27, 1952, p. 16.

to finish high school but were not too much interested in whether or not he went to college. His school marks were above average but not phenomenal like his IQ score. In mechanical drawing, however, he excelled his teacher in a few weeks' time. The teacher said that he should become a draftsman. This interested him but his community was not a large one. There were no jobs for draftsmen and neither he nor his parents knew where such training could be secured. The result was that when he finished high school, he got a job in a filling station; at last report he was still working there. Here was one who might have been a distinguished engineer or an architect, building schools and churches, rendering a service to society, but his abilities were never developed.

No one knows how many people have had unusual talent or outstanding ability and yet have never used it. One wonders how many store clerks might have been artists, how many Pullman porters might have been doctors, how many people are doing some monotonous job requiring only average ability who might have been leading ministers, educators, or statesmen if their talents had been recognized, trained, and developed. As James McKeen Cattell said some years ago, ". . . many a genius has been a 'mute inglorious Milton' lacking the character or the circumstance for the accomplishment of his task."[3] Many who possessed both high intelligence and special talent have created nothing. This problem is so real that a bulletin of Columbia University states that it results "in an estimated loss to society of at least half the people who have the capacity for making an outstanding contribution."[4]

[3] Quoted in Catherine Morris Cox, *The Early Mental Traits of Three Hundred Geniuses,* (Genetic Studies of Genius, vol. 2), Stanford University Press, 1926, p. 19.
[4] Passow, etc., *op. cit.,* p. 26.

This last statement is a sobering thought. It should be the concern of all. Our welfare, the future of the country depends upon how well this problem is faced and solved. It is not to minimize the importance of the people of average intelligence to say that advances, progress, and improvement depend, to a large degree, upon those who have exceptional ability, skill, and insight. Paul Witty, a recognized authority in the study of the gifted, says,

In our effort to banish serfdom and darkness from the world; in our effort to live in peace and prosperity with men everywhere, we need the best spiritual and creative leadership this country has to offer. . . . We need strong and free and courageous men and women to find new solutions to age-old problems. . . . We need the talent, the imagination, and the resourcefulness that only the gifted can bring to the solution of our problems and to the making of a better world.[5]

This is not meant to claim that the gifted are any better than others. Dr. D. A. Worcester points out that the gifted "are not better than, but different from, others."[6] They do have unusual ability that others do not have. They do have a contribution to make that others cannot make. They have a responsibility that others do not have. It has been said, "The maximum welfare for a group is achieved when each member of the group contributes as much as he is able."[7] This should be true of both the gifted and the retarded. We shall speak of the retarded later. Here we speak of the gifted. The challenge is to see that these gifted youth have the opportunity to develop their capacities to

[5] Paul Witty, *Helping the Gifted Child, Science* Research Associates, Chicago, 1953, pp. 47-8.

[6] Worcester, *The Education of Children of Above-Average Mentality,* University of Nebraska Press, 1956, p. 54.

[7] A statement of the Educational Policies Commission of the National Education Association, in *Education of the Gifted,* National Education Association, Washington, D. C., 1950, p. 2.

the full and to make the contribution they are capable of making.

Science and industry are making definite efforts to locate and to train gifted young people, however it is not only in science and industry that they are needed, but also in statesmanship, education, and social service. The church has much at stake in this search for outstanding talent. The church is confronted with a tragic shortage in positions of leadership. Much is said about recruitment for the ministry. Recruitment alone is not enough; there must be an effort to secure the best—in character, in ability, and in devotion to the task.

It is only to be realistic to recognize that most of these things we have been talking about are not being done now. On the contrary, as one writer points out, "The gifted child is too often the neglected child. Vast in capacity for response to stimulation, he is often left to his own devices to find an outlet for his talents."[8] Both Terman and Hollingsworth agreed that the gifted are likely to work far below their potential capacity. For this reason their unusual ability is often not even recognized. Those who have studied the problem from the standpoint of education consider them one of the most neglected groups in our public schools.[9] Baker, in his study of exceptional children, goes so far as to say, "As a matter of fact their exceptional abilities are so often unrecognized and their talents wasted that they are among the most handicapped of all groups."[10]

Special attention needs to be given this problem, not only by the schools but also by the churches and the com-

8 Nicholas Hobbs in *The Gifted Child*, American Association for Gifted Children, Paul Witty, Ed. D. C. Heath & Co., 1951, p. 163.
9 See Marion Scheifele, *The Gifted Child in the Regular Classroom*, Bureau of Publications, Teachers College, Columbia University, 1953, p. vii.
10 Harry J. Baker, *Introduction to Exceptional Children*, The Macmillan Company, 1947, p. 283.

munity as a whole. One of the basic principles of a democracy is equality of opportunity. Often this has been interpreted to mean identical opportunity, but, as has been said, "There is nothing so unequal as the equal treatment of unequals."[11] This has been recognized in some areas. It has often been pointed out that the handicapped and retarded need special attention in order to develop their capacities to the full. It has not been commonly recognized that the gifted need special opportunities to bring out their capacities to the full. Too often they are left to develop their talents in their own way. The result is a great waste in talent—and a great loss to society.

Our hope for the future depends upon the leadership, the skill, the ability, the desire to serve that we can arouse in the youth of today.

[11] Cf. Scheifele, *op. cit.*, p. 44.

Chapter II

Centuries of Indifference: The Historical Background

"The more extensive a man's knowledge of what has been done, the greater will be his power of knowing what to do." This statement of Disraeli's points out the fact that in any area of thought or action, it is practical first of all to gain some historical perspective, to see the problem in terms of its total picture, to be familiar with what others have done. Men have recognized the presence and also the importance of the gifted for a long time, but the actual study of the gifted has a very short history. Plato was conscious of this matter more than 2300 years ago and urged that those children who had unusual capacity should be trained for leadership in the state. He was convinced, even then, that Greek democracy would be no better than its leadership, and he advocated that superior youth should be selected and trained in science, philosophy, and metaphysics to become future leaders in the state. We have referred to Jesus' teachings in the parable of the talents and could cite other references which would indicate that He felt that those who have greater gifts have a greater responsibility. One of the most extensive efforts to locate and train gifted young people that is recorded in history was by a Mohammedan ruler, Suleiman the Magnificent, in the 16th century. He sent representatives throughout Asia Minor for the purpose of locating the most intelligent youth to be trained for the service of the empire.[1] This, however, was no attempt to study or understand the gifted.

Some men contend that all history is a record of the gifted. It is true that it includes the achievements and the activities of some gifted people. It even gives some information about their childhood and youth. We know that John Stuart Mill was reading Greek at the age of four; that Isaac Newton spent his childhood building working models of water clocks; and that Melanchthon received his bachelor's degree when he was fourteen and earned his master's degree, also; but was denied it because of his youthful appearance. History also reveals that the gifted are sometimes overlooked. Darwin is reported to have failed in his first course in zoology; when Pasteur finished the primary school in his home town of Arbois, he was rated only as a "good average" student. The story that Thomas Edison's teachers were unaware of his hearing handicap and considered him dull is legendary. History not only records the fact that brilliant men have been extolled and honored for their achievements but also that some have been misunderstood, maligned, and even persecuted because of their discoveries. Galileo had an understanding of the universe far in advance of his day, but, as a result, he was called before the Inquisition and faced severe punishment. Tyndall was a scholar of the first rank, but for his translation of the Scriptures into the language of the people he was burned at the stake. Brilliance and great ideas sometimes brought opposition instead of praise.

The attempt to understand and help the gifted is a product of the twentieth century, although there were instances before this. Karl Witte is reported to have been

[1] Cf. National Society for the Study of Education, *op. cit.,* p. 259.

trained to read five languages before he was nine, and Lord Kelvin received such training at home that he won distinctions at the University of Glasgow before he was twelve, but these were exceptions and represented no general attempt to train and help the gifted.

Prior to the twentieth century, there was practically no literature on the subject; no articles were written about it; no research projects were undertaken. The one exception was Sir Francis Galton who published his book on *Hereditary Genius* in 1869. He anticipated much that was to come later. Speaking of these people of great achievement, he said they are "always a feast to my eye, being as they are such massive, vigorous, capable looking animals."[2]

Only occasional attention was given to the problem by the schools. The whole educational philosophy of an earlier day worked against it. The thought of those who contended that all native intelligence was equal and that differences were due to training discouraged special attention to the gifted. Of course, many educators recognized that all children did not respond with the same results. Much more attention was given to those who had difficulty than to those to whom school work was easy. Many educators held to the philosophy that brilliant pupils would get along anyway and that teachers might better spend their time with those who needed help. About the turn of the century some schools began to make provisions for the gifted by permitting them to "skip" a grade in order to advance more rapidly; others placed them in groups utilizing what was called the three-track plan. In the 1920's special classes for the gifted were formed in such cities as Los Angeles, Cleveland, and Rochester, New York.

2 Galton, *Hereditary Genius*, Rev. ed. Appleton-Century-Crofts, 1891, pp. 331-2.

These were experimental and were not general throughout the country. A widespread interest in the problem had not arisen yet. Even as late as 1930, when a report of the White House Conference on Child Health and Protection appeared under the title, *Special Education—the Handicapped and the Gifted,* more than 515 pages were devoted to the handicapped and only 13 were given to the needs of the gifted student.[3]

Because of the work of Binet and his successors in providing intelligence tests by which a reasonably accurate objective measure of capacity would be made, the study of gifted children was extensively undertaken. Binet was commissioned to discover a means whereby retarded children could be recognized, but, in so doing, he likewise developed an instrument which made possible the recognition and identification of those who were gifted. His research made available an instrument by which the individual gifted child could be located and identified, and thus helped. It was also an instrument with which data could be secured about large groups of people, thus making possible extensive and accurate research.

The understanding of the gifted made its greatest forward step in 1921, when Lewis M. Terman, with an able staff of assistants, launched the Stanford Study of the Gifted. This is one of the most extended and exhaustive pieces of research into human behavior ever undertaken in America. The major portion of the project was a thorough study of some 1500 gifted children over a period of many years, for the purpose of determining the physical, mental, and personality traits that are characteristic of gifted children, and to find out by means of long-range follow-up how such

[3] Cf. American Association for Gifted Children, *op. cit.,* p. 4.

children develop and, as much as possible, what factors influence their development. There is no other source that contains as much information about gifted children and youth. For this reason it deserves consideration in some detail.

Terman had been much interested in general opinion regarding the bright and superior child. He found a common tendency to look upon the bright child with some misgiving. Many people felt that there was a close relationship between the brilliant and the abnormal; some even discouraged intellectual stimulation and development; teachers often disliked or resented the student with high IQ. Terman became more and more convinced that many common conceptions concerning the gifted child were wrong and that it was a subject of major social and educational importance. A grant from the Commonwealth Fund made it possible for him to undertake the monumental research.

There were several main features of the investigation which were determined at the start. It was not to be considered a direct attack upon the education of gifted children but was to be a search for information that would be of service to education in this hitherto unexplored field. They wanted to determine what physical, mental, and personality traits are typically characteristic of gifted children. The subjects selected for the study were to be as nearly as possible an unbiased sampling so that whatever would be true of this group would also be true of any other representative group. The procedures to be used were to be as objective as they could be, so that they could be checked and repeated. It was determined to follow the subjects as closely and as far into adult life as they could, thus to find out how such children develop and, if possible, what factors influence their later achievement. A companion study was proposed on the childhood of historical geniuses, which we will discuss a bit later.

The seriousness with which the project was undertaken is indicated by the care with which Terman selected his assistants. Recognizing that the success of the undertaking depended to a large extent on those who would be working with him, he visited the leading universities of the country searching for the most competent and well-trained. He was fortunate in securing for his two chief assistants Florence Goodenough, of Columbia, and Helen Marshall, of Ohio State. All those who worked on the project were given thorough training before they went into the field. The method they used in selecting their subjects is interesting in itself, but too lengthy to be included here. Suffice it to say that they selected 1,528 subjects from a total school population of about 250,000 in California. Most of the subjects were of 140 IQ, or above, selected because they were in the top one per cent of the population. The average intelligence for the pre-high school group was 131, and for the high school group 142.6.

They did not limit their investigation to the intelligence of these children. Eleven other areas were explored as well. A twelve-page, home-information sheet was filled out by parents. An eight-page, school-information sheet was filled out by each child's teacher. A one-hour medical examination was given to the majority of children and thirty-seven anthropometrical measurements were made. A three-hour battery of school achievement tests of general school subjects was given, not only to the gifted but to a control group as well. A battery of seven character tests was given to more than five hundred gifted children and an equal number in a control group. A four-page interest blank, giving interests in a wide variety of subjects, was filled out. A record of all books, with a rating by the children for degree of interest, and a test of play interest and patterns, a test on intellectual, social, and activity interests were all recorded. Home ratings were made by field workers in regard to both the homes and the neighborhoods of most of the subjects.

The study is obviously too extensive to report in detail here, but there are a few items of interest that should be included. Contrary to public opinion, the gifted children as a group were found to be above average in both height and weight, and, in all respects, slightly superior physically to other groups. There would be a few exceptions but the common stereotype of the bright child as being undersized and weak physically simply was not found to be true. As Terman states it, "The evidence obtained from anthropometric measurement, health histories, and medical examinations is unanimous and conclusive on this point."[4]

The educational achievement of the students was well above their chronological age. In grade placement they were found to be accelerated about 14 per cent for their age, but in mastery of subject matter they were accelerated about 44 per cent. As a general rule, the gifted children were more interested in "abstract" subjects in school, less interested in the "practical" fields, but they expressed about the same degree of interest as other children in games and sports. "Although there are exceptions to the rule, the typical gifted child likes active games, plays with tools and machinery, likes the companionship of others, and shows

4 Lewis M. Terman and others, *The Gifted Child Grows Up*, (Genetic Studies of Genius, Vol. 4), Stanford University Press, 1947, p. 55.

no abnormal fondness for study and solitude."[5] The gifted children showed more maturity in their play interests and they were much more inclined to make collections.

Early indications of intelligence were quick understanding, insatiable curiosity, extensive information, retentive memory, large vocabulary, and unusual facility at reading. The interests of gifted children were found to be many-sided and spontaneous. In terms of interests, the gifted children manifested a great superiority in intellectual interests; their differences were not quite so great in social interests, while in activity interests the two groups were about the same.

The results of character tests were quite decisive. The gifted group scored "better" than the control group in all tests administered.[6] These included such tests as honesty, social attitudes, and emotional stability. They were found to be less inclined to boast, although their achievement in most cases exceeded others. They were less inclined to cheat on school examinations and their social attitudes were found to be more wholesome.

Terman, in summarizing the results of these findings, pointed out two facts which seemed to stand out and which were of major importance: (1) The deviation of the gifted from the general population is in the upward direction for nearly all traits. This is another way of saying that desirable traits tend to be positively rather than negatively correlated. There is no law of compensation whereby the intellectual superiority of the gifted is sure to be offset by inferiorities along nonintellectual lines. (2) The amount of upward deviation is not the same in all traits. It is greatest in those aspects of behavior most closely related to intelligence,

[5] *Ibid.*, p. 53.
[6] See *Ibid.*, p. 47

such as originality, intellectual interests, and ability to score high in achievement tests.[7] He further warns, however, that all these findings are of a composite picture; there are many exceptions and a wide range of variability with individual gifted children within the group.

One of the most significant features of Terman's study was the fact that he was able to follow up his group over the years. Six years after the initial study a grant from the Commonwealth Fund made it possible for him to undertake a follow-up study. Three full-time assistants were secured who spent an entire year testing children and interviewing parents and teachers. The results of this study are reported in the third volume of the series, *The Promise of Youth: Follow-Up Studies of a Thousand Gifted Children*.[8] The one most important outcome of the follow-up study was that "the composite portrait of the group had changed only in minor respects in six years."[9]

Even the six-year follow-up did not complete the study. A part-time assistant was employed to keep in touch with the group by correspondence. In 1936 a fairly extensive survey was made by mail, securing such information as educational progress, health, achievements, activities of parents, and so forth. A more extensive follow-up was made possible in 1940 and in 1945 as a result of a very generous grant from the Carnegie Corporation and some other gifts. This made it possible to secure the services of assistants and research associates to carry on the project. The subjects were now 35 to 36 years of age (average) and it was possible to discover to some extent how gifted chil-

[7] *Ibid.*, p. 57.
[8] By Burks, Jensen and Terman, (Genetic Studies of Genius, Vol. 3), Stanford University Press, 1930.
[9] *Ibid.*, p. 64.

dren progress and turn out. Of course, by this time it also
called for the co-operation of husbands and wives. Information was desired now that had not been included in the
previous studies, such as vocational interest and achievement, marital adjustment, record of children, and so forth.
Obviously, the locating, contacting, checking, testing,
securing information from such a large group by now
widely scattered was a tremendous undertaking. The co-
operation of the gifted subjects (they can no longer be
called gifted children) was exceedingly good. Around 96
per cent coverage was secured, which was amazing in itself.
No other such follow-up study has ever been made.

The study was published in the fourth volume of the
series, *The Gifted Child Grows Up: Twenty-five Years
Follow-up of a Superior Group*.[10] This volume included a
summary of all previous studies as an introduction to the
findings of the follow-up study. It is undoubtedly the most
significant single volume in the field thus far.

It was found that the group still excels the general population in averages of height and weight. Their health
record was above average. Their mortality rate was only
four fifths of the normal expectation. Educational histories
indicated that attendance at college and university was
about eight times as great as it was for the general population of California. Ninety per cent of the men and eighty-
six per cent of the women attended college; 70 per cent
of the men and 67 per cent of the women graduated. Graduate degrees were received by 51 per cent of the men and
21 per cent of the women. In terms of occupational status
about 45 per cent were in the professional fields, more than

10 Terman and others, (Genetic Studies of Genius, Vol. 4), Stanford University Press,
1947.

25 per cent in semiprofessional, a little more than 20 per cent in clerical and skilled trades. Only 1.29 per cent were in agriculture, 6.22 per cent in semiskilled trades, and only .69 per cent were in slightly skilled trades and none were employed as day laborers. The percentage in the professions was larger than that of their parents and eight times larger than that of the general population. During the depression, when 15-20 per cent of men in California were unemployed, only 1 per cent of this group was unemployed.

In terms of such matters as interest and avocational activities, there were no norms by which they could compare the group with the general population, but the research would indicate a very wide range of such interests. Most studies have found this to be a characteristic of the gifted. Only rarely do they concentrate their attention on a single line of activity. Sports received the most frequent mention by both men and women, followed by such items as photography, music, gardening, reading, collections, woodworking, and writing.[11]

There are many other findings that are of interest and value. The emotional maturity and social adjustment, as nearly as it could be measured, was very high. As Terman pointed out, there was no yardstick for measuring such intangibles as happiness, but there was less mental disease and fewer cases of suicide recorded than for the general population. The incidence of delinquency was extremely low. The marriage rate equals that of the general population and the marital adjustment would compare favorably with that of the general population. Intelligence tests administered in 1940 gave a mean score a standard deviation above the average of college graduates, verifying the rule

11 *Ibid.*, 205.

that "intellectually superior children become intellectually superior adults."[12]

This project has been reported at some length because it is such an outstanding example of careful, thorough, painstaking research and because it is the greatest single source of information that we have about the gifted and because the findings are of real significance to the pastor and religious educator as they work with youth.

Another part of Terman's study, but so different that it can almost be called a parallel study, was a study of the childhood and youth of famous men, by Catherine Cox. It was proposed that along with Terman's study of gifted youth, there should be a companion study of the childhood of historical geniuses to compare them with the group of living superior children. Miss Cox carried out the study under the direction of Dr. Terman. She, in turn, had a corps of assistants working under her. Others, like Galton, Cattell, and William James, had studied the lives of great men before this, but none as exhaustively as this. The data when assembled amounted to six thousand pages of typewritten material. When it appeared in book form, under the title *The Early Mental Traits of Three Hundred Geniuses*, it amounted to 842 pages, including fifty-nine tables and graphs.

Miss Cox searched biographies in English, French, and German, selecting 301 of the most eminent men and women in history, from 1450 to 1850, and gathered what data she could about their heredity, childhood, and youth. In one sense this just reversed the procedure of Terman. He selected his subjects in childhood and followed them through to maturity, and she selected her subjects on the

---

12 National Society for the Study of Education, *op. cit.*, p. 273.

basis of adult achievement and sought information about their earlier experiences. The type of things she and her staff investigated were their earliest educational experiences, when they first began to read, and the extent and nature of their reading. They sought information about things they wrote, created, and produced, and any precocious activities. They studied any mathematical performances, and the recognition of similarities or differences. All such things could be compared with intelligence-test findings. They tried to discover any unusually intelligent applications of knowledge, any early maturity of attitude and judgment, any tendency to discriminate or theorize. They gathered information about their interests, their school status, their progress, and their family standing.[13]

Many of the biographies did not give information that could be compared with established norms, but on the basis of what material they had they determined an estimated IQ for each person; one was the IQ which the material indicated he might have scored in childhood, and another was the IQ which he might have scored in youth. Of interest to readers of this volume would be the findings in terms of some of the individuals who were studied. About sixteen per cent were religious leaders and philosophers. The IQ ratings estimated for some of them were as follows:

Name	Childhood IQ	Youth IQ
John Bunyan	105	120
George Fox	110	120
Martin Luther	115	145
Thomas Cranmer	120	130
Johann Sebastian Bach	125	140
Theodore Beza	125	140

13 Cf. Cox, *op. cit.*, p. 41.

Name	Childhood IQ	Youth IQ
John Locke	125	135
Lancelot Andrewes	135	140
Richard Baxter	135	135
Ludwig van Beethoven	135	140
John Calvin	135	150
Desiderius Erasmus	135	140
Immanuel Kant	135	150
William Penn	135	150
William Robertson	135	140
John Wesley	135	140
Ulrich Zwingli	140	140
Thomas Chalmers	145	160
William Ellery Channing	145	150
Ralph Waldo Emerson	145	145
George Frederick Handel	145	155
John Milton	145	170
George W. Hegel	150	145
Wolfgang Mozart	150	155
Friedrich Schleiermacher	150	145
Philipp Melanchthon	160	180
Blaise Pascal	180	180
Johan Wolfgang Goethe	185	200

She drew three interesting conclusions as a result of her study: (1) *"Youths who achieve eminence have, in general, (a) a heredity above the average and (b) superior advantages in early environment."*[14] This is not always true. Abraham Lincoln and Charles Dickens, for example, did not have superior advantages in early environment, but it is usually true. (2) *"Youths who achieve eminence are distinguished in childhood by behavior which indicates an unusually high IQ.*[15] In other words, early in life there are usually indications of superior ability that predict or foreshadow

14 *Ibid.*, p. 215.
15 *Ibid.*, pp. 216-17.

later performance. (3) Achievement is not a result of intellectual ability alone but also of other factors, such as interest, effort, persistence, and character. ". . . . *Youths who achieve eminence are characterized not only by high intellectual traits, but also by persistence of motive and effort, confidence in their abilities, and great strength or force of character.*"[16] Speaking of persistence, she said, ". . . . *High but not the highest intelligence, combined with the greatest degree of persistence, will achieve greater eminence than the highest degree of intelligence with somewhat less persistence.*"[17]

Another person who made a major contribution to an understanding of the gifted child was Professor Leta S. Hollingworth, of Columbia University. Interestingly enough, she came into the field of the gifted by way of the retarded child. She was serving as clinical psychologist at Bellevue Hospital, where it was her task to test mentally inferior children for commitment by the court.[18] While she was teaching a course at Columbia Teachers College on the psychology of the subnormal child, she gave a test to a superior child as a demonstration of the contrast that existed. She continued to work with the boy who registered the very unusual IQ score of 187, and her attention was gradually turned from the lower end of the scale to the top level of distribution.

Her help was solicited more and more frequently for mentally gifted children who had educational or personal problems. The problem of placing a seven-year-old boy who was far superior to the others in his public school

16 *Ibid.,* p. 218.
17 *Ibid.,* p. 187.
18 See "The Contributions of Leta S. Hollingworth," by Miriam C. Pritchard, American Association for Gifted Children, *op. cit.,* p. 47ff.

class led to her experiments with gifted children and her relationship with the public schools. Her efforts consisted of "highly organized educational experiments which she herself conceived, planned, and supervised in every detail. . . ."[19] The total number with which she worked was only a little over 100 but she worked intensively with them, observing them almost every school day and maintaining contact with them personally beyond their school experience.

It was in 1916 that she gave the test to the gifted child and had her attention turned to this problem. It was in 1922 that she formed her two Special Opportunity classes. These classes were formed because of the feeling that "there are children with such markedly superior mental ability that no regular classroom can hope to meet their needs."[20] Two classes were formed, one with an IQ of 150 and above on the Stanford Binet Test, the other with an IQ from 134 to 154. The stated purposes were: "First, the particular children in it must be educated—the class exists for them; but secondly, they must be studied—our knowledge of such children must be increased, for we have, after all, very little information to guide us. . . ."[21] Professor Hollingworth herself pursued information about every aspect of the life of the gifted child that could be discovered.

In 1934 the New York schools, in an attempt to meet the need for individualization of instruction, organized Public School 500, the Speyer School, to solve two major problems, the education of the slow learner and the education for the intellectually gifted. The classes for slow learners were called the Binet classes because of the con-

19 *Ibid.,* p. 48.
20 *Ibid.,* p. 55.
21 *Ibid.,* p. 55.

tribution of Binet to backward children. The classes for gifted children were called Terman classes and consisted of pupils who scored above 130 IQ. Professor Hollingworth was assigned to work with the Terman classes. She was especially interested in children with an IQ above 180, who occur only once or twice in a million. In twenty-three years of searching in metropolitan New York and testing literally thousands of children, she located only twelve who tested at this level. As a result of her experiences, careful and extensive observation, and controlled studies, she came to many conclusions and revealed some significant findings.

Her findings were largely the result of individual contact and observation. She was more interested in the individual than in statistical research. As a result, she did not attempt studies involving large numbers of subjects. She personally followed some of the students through fifteen years after their school experience.

She found that some gifted children needed only half the usual time to cover the prescribed subjects and some of the very high group needed only one fourth as much time. This left them with a great deal of time that could be used for other material. It was her judgment that

Children up to about 140 IQ tolerate the ordinary school routine fairly well, being usually a little young for their grades . . . and achieve excellent marks without serious effort. But above this status, children become increasingly bored with school work, if kept in or nearly in the lock step.[22]

The result is that they may regard school with indifference or distaste for they "find nothing interesting to do there." What are the implications for the church school?

[22] *Ibid.*, 73-74.

Another problem which she recognized was the lack of congenial companionship for gifted children with children of their own age. This created a problem in social adjustment. Since there were so few children at the top level of intelligence, it was difficult for them to find friends of their own age group with the same interests and understandings. She felt that one prerequisite for any teacher of the gifted was the ability to realize that gifted students "often have more information and deeper insights into a topic than she herself can have." She felt that unless the teacher recognized this fact she would come into conflict with the student and not realize the possibilities of such work.[23]

Professor Hollingworth did not like the term "genius" as applied to gifted children. Others had spoken of children above 140 IQ as geniuses, but she contended that this term should be used only in reference to those individuals who had made outstanding contributions of lasting worth. She preferred the term "potential genius," feeling that only time could tell whether or not they had sufficient initiative, industry, and perseverance to deserve the term of genius.[24]

There have been many misconceptions of the talented and some prejudice against them. She believed that this attitude was the reflection of "widespread resentment of the more able by the less able."[25] She was particularly concerned about the gifted young people who had great promise but did not have the means to secure an education. Very frequently she approached foundations and philanthropic agencies to set up scholarship funds, but she was usually refused. She found it was much easier to secure funds for dependent children. The attitude she usually

23 *Ibid.*, p. 63.
24 *Ibid.*, p. 72.
25 *Ibid.*, p. 89.

met was that the gifted children should take care of themselves.

She continually stressed that these children have a unique contribution to make to society. As much as anyone else, she was conscious of the loss to mankind as a result of the failure to develop the potentialities of these superior children. She felt we were just at the beginning of this work and did not yet know what our responsibilities toward these gifted children were.[26]

The work of these pioneers did much to make others aware of both the problems and the possibilities of the gifted. Along with Terman and Hollingworth, others, like Paul Witty, at Northwestern University, Dean A. Worcester, of the University of Nebraska, and Ruth Strang, of Columbia University, began to study the gifted. We shall be referring to these people frequently in this volume.

The publication of Terman's studies stimulated others to write. Articles began to appear in educational journals, even in popular magazines. Texts on special education and on the psychology of exceptional children gave the gifted a much larger place. Teachers colleges included courses in the education of the gifted. Graduate students in psychology and education began to do research in the area of the gifted. Schools everywhere began to recognize the problem and to discuss the relative merits of grouping, acceleration, and enrichment. We shall discuss these plans in more detail when we come to the chapter, "The Religious Education of the Gifted." Our point here is that the problem was recognized by the educational world and efforts were being made to solve it.

The International Council of Exceptional Children

[26] *Ibid.*, p. 54.

was organized and had for its main purpose the improving of educational opportunities for exceptional children, which included the gifted. The American Association for Gifted Children was a national organization created to give exclusive attention to the gifted child. Their purposes are to create a more widespread understanding of the nature of the gifted, to improve all phases of education, teaching, curriculum and research. Their publication committee has produced one excellent colume, *The Gifted Child,* edited by Paul Witty, with a very excellent list of contributors.

One thing that has been very noticeable in this chapter is that there has been almost no mention of the church. The reason for that is that the church has given very little attention to the subject. It is true that in programs of recruitment for the ministry stress has been laid upon finding the finest and most capable young people, but there has been little or no attempt to study or to understand them. There have been several books on the education of the gifted, but no books on the religious education of the gifted. As was stated in the Introduction, there have been studies of the psychology of religion and many books and articles on pastoral counseling, but almost none in the problems and needs of the gifted or on the pastor and his relationship to the gifted. This is an area that needs to receive much attention.

Chapter III

Understanding Gifted Youth: The Psychology of the Gifted

The purpose of the church in considering the gifted is twofold. First, it is to challenge them, to help them develop so that they can make the contribution they ought to make. Second, it is to help them, for they, too, have problems and needs. One is just as important as the other, but if we are to do either we must understand these people. The first step in either case is to learn all we can about them. For this reason we have included a chapter on the psychology of the gifted, although we recognize that the very title presents us with an impossible task. Psychology itself is a very broad term; it includes everything that is known about human nature, human behavior, the mind, the emotions, the environment, social relations, growth and development, etc., etc. This cannot all be included in one volume, let alone one chapter. To discuss the psychology of the gifted is even more difficult. Much research still needs to be done. In fact, Ruth Strang says, "The dynamic psychology of gifted children is still to be written."[1] Yet much has already been discovered, and we can at least point to some of the findings that have already been made clear.

[1] From *Psychology of Exceptional Children and Youth*, by Cruickshank, Prentice Hall, 1955, p. 475.

How Does One Identify the Gifted?

One of the first questions the pastor will face is, "How do you identify them?" He might well say, "Granted we need to challenge them and we are perfectly willing to help them, how do we know who they are? If we have 100, 200, 500 children in church school; if we have 10, 20, 40 or 50 in a youth fellowship, how can we tell which ones are gifted?" It is not easy. The gifted child is not easily identified. As a matter of fact, his appearance is so much like that of anyone else that he is often overlooked entirely.

Observation is our first opportunity. We have them in our church programs. We have the chance to observe them in various activities. But what should we look for? Vocabulary is probably the first clue. The language of the gifted is usually far in advance of that of others of his age. Witty tells of a gifted boy and his aunt who were caught out in a boat on a lake. As night was coming on, the boy appealed to a fisherman in a near-by boat. "Mr. Fisherman," he said, "would it be possible for you to extricate us from this predicament we have become involved in?" The fisherman paid no attention until the aunt said, "What he means is, will you get us out of this mess?"[2] As we observe a young person in a church school class or in the discussion period of a youth meeting, we can watch for evidences of superior mental capacity.

The gifted child tends to possess a superior ability in reasoning, in generalizing, in solving problems, in understanding abstract subjects and discovering meanings. He learns more rapidly and easily, and shows more intellectual curiosity. He can work independently, shows much origin-

[2] From Witty, *op. cit.*, 1952, p. 24.

ality, exhibits alertness and quickness of response. There are exceptions where gifted children do not exhibit some of these qualities, but when the qualities are present, it is a good indication of superior ability. However, the pastor working with a young person will not base a judgment on his own observation alone. If there is a question of vocational choice, for example, when the decision might require four or more years of college training, he should not guess as to whether or not the person has the capacity to fulfill the requirements of such a choice.

What other sources of information are available? The school is one of the best and certainly the most available. The teachers who see the young person every day have an opportunity to gain an evaluation of his abilities that is not accessible to the pastor. Teachers are usually willing to co-operate with a pastor in helping to provide guidance for a young person in whom both are interested. Needless to say, a pastor goes to a teacher not to gain confidential information but to gain a better understanding of the young person he is trying to help.

It should be pointed out that the teacher's judgment can be wrong. Teachers are human and are subject to the same errors we all are. One teacher may consider a certain pupil bright; another teacher may consider the same pupil average. The child who behaves well, causes no difficulty in class, and makes a good appearance may be judged higher than the one who causes some difficulty. Actually the second may have more actual ability than the first. An older child in a class of younger children is sometimes considered brighter when he has really had more experience. Class achievement and grades are often confused with ability. Even though achievement and ability are directly related, many children of ability do not achieve because of other complicating factors or the lack of motivation. All such things should be kept in mind; yet the fact remains that the teacher has the opportunity to evaluate the student's abilities from a wider perspective than anyone else, and years of experience help to eliminate such errors as we have mentioned here. It also should serve to make the pastor more cautious. If teachers can be wrong in their judgments, how much more easily can those who have not had the same training and experience.

Another clue to intellectual capacity is the grades a student receives in school. Good school marks usually indicate a good intelligence. There are exceptions. Grades are a result of teachers' judgments and so are subject to all the errors mentioned in the paragraphs above. Several studies have been made that show how very subjective grades can be. One hundred English teachers were asked to study the same composition and give it a grade in terms of percentage and indicate the school year in which they would expect that quality of work to be done. The percentage grades ranged from 60 to 98, and the estimated grade location varied from the fifth grade to the junior year in college. It was found that a group of college instructors assigned different marks to their own papers when they regraded them without knowledge of the former marks they had given. Such illustrations are not included to destroy our confidence in grades but to make us cautious about making a decision on something as subjective as grades.

The quiet, obedient, friendly child is more likely to receive good grades than the independent thinking, active child who asks difficult questions and may at times become bored or cause a disturbance. Yet his questions, even his boredom, may be an indication of superior ability. For these reasons grades from several teachers, or over a period of several years are a better clue to ability than are grades from one teacher for one semester. Consistently good grades are a good indication of superior ability when we recognize that grades are highly subjective.

It does not always follow that poor grades are an indication of poor intelligence. In most cases that would be true, but not always. Here is the example of a boy who seemed to make no progress at all in school. The principal, feeling that something should be done for the lad, recommended a Binet intelligence test as a routine measure before assigning him to a class for mentally retarded children. The result of the test was an intelligence quotient of 145. If the boy had been judged by the teacher's evaluation or by his grades, he would have been considered a retarded child; actually he was highly gifted.[3]

For the reasons cited above, achievement tests are more accurate than grades. They were designed to counteract the subjective nature of grading and to make available tests of educational achievement standardized on a wide sampling of the population and usable in many schools at the same time. They are created to measure how much a person has learned from an educational experience. Some tests measure achievement in a single subject and some cover wide areas of learning. Usually there is a high correlation between achievement test scores and school marks. They are particularly useful in detecting the gifted. On occasion it may be found that a student who has seemingly been paying little attention in class actually has achieved a great

[3] Reported in National Society for the Study of Education, *op. cit.*, p. 253.

deal of knowledge and information in some area. While his grades may be average, his actual achievement may be a grade or two beyond the class, by objective standardized measures. As yet no such standardized tests have been developed for religious education.

The best single measure of intellectual ability is the standard intelligence test, as was stated in the Introduction. That is the only means that would have revealed the true ability of the boy mentioned above. When there is a question of intellectual capacity, the score of a standardized test should be secured. But this is a book designed for ministers and other religious workers. Where can they get such a score? First, we should mention where he should not get it. He should not take an individual's word that he had an IQ of such and such a figure at school, or the words of a parent that John or Jane has an IQ at the top of the class. All such information has too many chances for error.

In most schools standardized intelligence tests are given as a routine procedure. Some form of an intelligence test is given on entrance to any college or university. There is a difference of opinion as to whether such information should be made available to anyone outside of the school. This, as in all matters of referral and interprofessional relationships, must follow a strict code of ethics. Such information should not be sought without the consent of the individual concerned. When a pastor has a good relationship with a young person he is counseling, that person is usually quite willing for him to talk to school authorities and to see his school records. The school authorities also have the obligation to know the one to whom they make available such information and the purposes for which it is to be used. It is highly doubtful whether or not an exact

IQ score should ever be given, but we see no reason why a person's capacity in terms of general areas, such as gifted, average, retarded, etc., cannot be made available—provided the information is used professionally, confidentially, and for the good of the student.

The pastor should be aware that in the average high school the tests that are given are group tests. Group tests are valuable to serve as a screening device and to give a general picture, but they are not as accurate as an individual test. When a question arises, an individual test, like the Stanford-Binet or the Wechsler-Bellevue, is always a good procedure. Where can such tests as these be secured? Larger school systems, colleges, and universities usually have a psychologist who can administer such tests. Most state universities have departments in which such tests can be secured for a modest fee. In some communities child guidance centers have such services available for a flexible fee, depending upon the financial condition of the individual or his family.

It should be remembered that two people with the same total score may differ considerably in the nature of that ability. Two gifted young people, both with high IQ's, may differ in the areas of greatest strength. One may score high on items of a verbal nature but the other on numerical or space items.

It must also be reiterated that intelligence tests are not infallible. The child's attitude, his motivation, his physical condition, his relationship with the tester can all influence his efforts. When there is a question as to result, a retest is always a good procedure. One should check more closely when the score is low than when it is high; that is, there are many reasons why a person may do less than he is capable of—lack of interest, poor health, distracting influences, etc.—but there is no way that he can do better than he is capable of, except to be lucky and he can't be lucky on all of the items.

In spite of its limitations the intelligence test is the one most effective single instrument for measuring and selecting the individual of superior mental ability.

Intelligence tests identify only intellectual ability. They are most effective in measuring "scholastic aptitude," and in predicting academic success. They do not measure motivation, interest, or character. They do not discover the gifted in such areas as the arts, creativity, or leadership ability. For discovering those with special talents in these areas we are still quite dependent upon observation. The pastor is in a unique position to discover those with leadership ability. He can observe the young person in relation with the group and can offer him tryout experiences in a variety of activities.

Performance is still the final criterion. If test score or teachers' judgments say a person cannot do something and performance proves he can, then the judgments and even the tests must be wrong. "The final proof of genius is found in the work which genius produces."[4] All these methods of identifying the gifted supplement each other and should be considered together—observation, teachers' judgments, and the judgments of other persons who have the chance to observe the subjects, grades, achievement test scores, intelligence test scores, and performance. Taken together, they give quite an accurate picture of the abilities of a child or young person.

[4] Elise H. Martens, *Curriculum Adjustment for Gifted Children*, Washington, United States Government Printing Office, 1946.

Where Are They Found?

Where are the gifted found? The real answer to this question is that they may be found anywhere. Terman, in studying the homes and family background of his subjects, found that a little more than 31 per cent came from the professional group, about 50 per cent from the semiprofessional and business group, a little more than 11 per cent from the skilled group, and about 6 per cent from homes in which the father was engaged in semiskilled or unskilled labor. Other studies have been made that would bear this out, that the majority come from homes that represent the professional or semiprofessional vocations. It should also be pointed out that these homes provide not only a favorable heredity but also a favorable environment. They are usually surrounded with books, magazines, opportunities for travel, participation in organizations and activities—all of which contribute to the kind of experience that shows up well on an intelligence test. These studies also reveal that the gifted can be discovered anywhere, in the city, in the country, from wealthy parents or from poor; they are found in every race and every cultural group. How many children of real talent go unrecognized and undeveloped because of a barren home, an uncreative environment, or a lack of opportunity, no one knows. History reveals this fact: Washington was the child of a wealthy family; Lincoln lived in what might be called a lean-to log cabin. John Stuart Mill had a well-known and eminent father; Shakespeare was the child of a man who could not write his own name. From the standpoint of the pastor, the point is that gifted children may be found anywhere, in any community, in any parish.

What Are the Characteristics of the Gifted?

When Terman began his study, there were many common misconceptions and stereotypes that were widely held concerning the gifted. There are some that still exist—and ought to be overcome. They are not peculiar, physically weak, or unusual in appearance. The story is told of a boy who went into a bookstore and inquired about a book on science. The clerk tried to send him to the children's section, but he insisted that he wanted something on atomic energy, particularly something that explained the structure of the uranium isotope U-235. After examining several volumes, he selected the one he wanted, thanked the clerk, and went out. After he left the owner of the book store exclaimed, "Whew!—a real child prodigy, but he seemed like a nice kid, not at all what you'd expect."[5]

The question is, what should one expect? The common caricature, which the clerk no doubt had in mind, is of someone with thick glasses, a weak body; someone a bit queer, who does not associate with his fellows. Many people feel that a high mental ability is usually associated with poor physical and social qualities. As a matter of fact, research like Terman's has pointed out that in the main the opposite is true. While there are some instances in which this may be the case, the majority would be both physically and socially equal or superior to the average.

Actually there is no such thing as a typical gifted child or youth. There is no pattern that is common to all. They display an infinite variety of patterns and each one is unique in his own right. There are certain characteristics

[5] American Association for Gifted Children, *op. cit.*, p. 3.

that are common to most of the gifted. Some of these we have already indicated.

One of the most evident characteristics is his interest in reading and his superior reading ability. Most of the research that has been done has found that the majority of gifted children are inveterate readers. They begin to read earlier and usually have a wider range of reading interests. They turn to adult books and magazines much sooner, and frequently do extensive reading in certain fields. They spend much more time in reading than do others of their age; some authorities estimate as much as three times as much. This interest in reading seems to be evident at all ages of development.

The gifted child tends to have superior powers of generalization. He can see underlying principles more quickly. He is able to recognize relationships, to comprehend meanings, to think logically. He has greater powers of concentration. He can sustain attention longer than the average and very much longer than the retarded.

The gifted youth has much more originality, much greater initiative, and a wider curiosity. A very common characteristic is his wide range of interests. All studies of the activities and hobbies of the gifted reveal that this is true. While he enjoys the same games and sports that average children enjoy, he is much more interested in such thing as musical instruments, collections, atlases, and encyclopedias, usually without outside stimulation.

Socially and emotionally the gifted as a group show superiority in desirable traits. There are, of course, exceptions but in the main they are more courteous, willing to take suggestions, able to get along with others, and they have a keener sense of humor. As a group they are above average in such character traits as honesty and dependability.

Gifted youth are chosen as leaders more often than average or dull children—up to a certain point. It does not seem to be the case with the top one or two per cent with IQ's of 150 and over. The ideas and interests of these children are so different from those of their peers that they are not selected for places of leadership. Youth with very high IQ's are more likely to work and play alone than with others.

What Are Their Needs?

The needs of mentally gifted children are the same as the needs of any other children. They need acceptance, affection, and attention. They need a feeling of belongingness, a sense of security, a sense of achievement and personal worth. They need to be loved and understood. Because the gifted child has superior ability and can do superior work does not mean that he always has a sense of achievement or a sense of worth. On the contrary, he may have a feeling of frustration as great or greater than that of the handicapped. It should always be remembered that he is much like other children, with the same physical, emotional, and social needs and desires. As with other children and young people, these needs must be met if he is to develop a wholesome, balanced personality. When these normal and basic desires do not find satisfaction, then problems arise.

Modern psychology of adolescence speaks of "developmental tasks." These begin in infancy and continue throughout life. The infant has the task of learning to walk, which enables him to get about and reveals a new area of experience. He has the task of securing a language by which he can communicate with others. He has the task of learning to read which opens up a whole new world. The adolescent has the task of finding his place in the world of work, of selecting the vocation by which he will earn his living, through which he will find many of life's satisfactions and in which he will make his contribution to society. He has the task of gaining an understanding of the opposite sex and of his own relationship with them. He has the task of gaining a philosophy of life, an interpretation of the universe, and an understanding of the world in which he lives and the meaning of life itself. The gifted face all these developmental tasks. They must acquire all the skills and tools of learning required for living in this complicated society that we have today. They sometimes encounter unique problems, as well. They have special and unusual interests that demand satisfaction. They have great capacity that needs to be recognized and challenged. Although it is important to provide special opportunities so that these unusual abilities can be expressed, it is equally important that the gifted child be allowed to be a child, to have opportunity for normal play experiences that parallel the development of any special abilities. He needs to develop a faith to live by. No amount of brilliance can take the place of a deep, underlying faith that supports, guides, and strengthens life.

What Are Their Problems?

If we are to help the gifted youth find his place in life, if we are to help him find personal satisfaction and make the contribution of which he is capable, we must understand some of the problems he is likely to face. We should know some of the areas of difficulty that will present themselves to the teacher of the church school class or the sponsor of the youth group of which he is a member. Both children and young people of superior ability have all the normal problems of growing up that are common to all youth. In addition, they are sometimes (not always) confronted with problems or difficulties the average child does not meet. Some of their problems are intensified by their superior ability. While their high intelligence gives them insights which are helpful in solving many problems, it also can be the source of a keen sensitivity that makes them aware of problems that might not present themselves to another at all.

A child's very giftedness may result in bad academic habits. Since he is capable of grasping his assignments quickly and with little effort, he sits idly by while others are attempting to complete what he has already accomplished. Such a situation can lead to several results. He can accept the situation quietly with bored indifference. More likely, he will turn his energy to something else and get into mischief, bother other students, and alienate the teacher. Some may rebel against school work and school authorities. Others may develop attitudes of conceit or smugness toward those who are unable to keep up with them. This can present a real problem when the student goes on to college. When his work came so easily in high school, he may not have developed good study and work habits and then at the university level he finds himself in competition with other young people of ability equal to his. He finds he is no longer at the head of the class and achievement here requires time, effort, and concentration such as he has never given before. At times this is a rather difficult adjustment to make.

Many of the problems faced by the gifted are caused not by the child's superiority but by the reactions of other people to that superiority. When a young person is recognized as brilliant, when he is consistently able to excel others in the classroom or in a discussion group, it does not always help his relationship with other young people, or even with adults. Many resent his superior ability, some are jealous, some openly hostile. The above average person is often shunned by the average and, on occasion, ridiculed and criticized.

One of the greatest problems that the gifted faces is his relationship with others. A study of Columbia University Teachers College tells the story of a boy named Jim. He had an IQ of 140. He was a prodigious reader with an excellent scholastic record. Both his knowledge and his interests were much wider than were those of the rest of the class. Because of his information and his interest he tended to dominate most of the discussion in class. The rest of the class began to tire of his continued superiority and to resent the teacher's praise of his work.

As his classmates began to shun him he turned to older children in an attempt to establish new relationships, but these relationships did not last. The older boys showed some interest in the things he had, like his home science laboratory, but they did not include him in their games and activities. He was both younger and smaller and could not compete with them in athletics. Neither his own age group nor the older group included him on informal occasions and he was frequently observed to be alone during lunch hour.

A boy may react to a situation like Jim's in a variety of ways. He may withdraw farther and continue his interests alone. He may become more arrogant, looking down upon other people and alienating himself even more. He may even attempt to do his school work poorly in order to identify himself more closely with other students. Gifted students have been known to attempt to conceal their ability by deliberate nonachievement rather than lose the approval of the group. Some of Terman's subjects admitted that they developed a "loathing for the reputation they had acquired of being intellectually highbrow and, in some cases, admitted . . . they had often feigned ignorance in their classes in order to appear more like their fellows."[6] As one gifted girl said, "It's bad enough to be taller than the boys, but when you're brighter, too, it's fatal."[7]

All of this serves to point out that one of the areas in which the gifted may find the greatest source of difficulty is in social relations. Even as a small child his play patterns and interests may vary from those of other children. He wants to organize play into more complicated patterns and is not interested in simple games that may appeal to other children. As gifted children get older, they may find difficulty in communicating with their less-gifted school-mates. Children with unusual mental ability want to be like others and have friends, just as other children do, but their very giftedness may separate them from others. A person usually chooses his friends because they have interests in common. It has frequently been pointed out that congeniality between persons depends upon their ability to think of the same things, to talk of the same things, and to be interested in the same things. This poses a problem for the gifted. His ideas are frequently not

6 Terman, *op. cit.*, p. 158.
7 Quoted by Strang in American Association for Gifted Children, *op. cit.*, p. 142.

understood by his classmates, his use of language is too advanced, his vocabulary is different, his interests are not shared, and he is likely to look on some of the activities of his classmates as trifling or unimportant. A girl of thirteen loved art and music and enjoyed visiting museums and the theater. One day she said to her mother, "Do you think I'll ever have a friend?" Her mother, taken by surprise, said, "But you do have friends." The girl replied, "No, Mother, I mean a real friend, someone I can talk to, who likes the same things I like."[8]

The higher the intellectual ability the more difficult it may become to adapt to the more ordinary interests and activities of others. Ruth Strang describes the plight of the gifted, "Weary of thinking, playing, and working on the relatively immature level of his chronological equals, he tends to withdraw from social contacts and devote himself to his own more satisfying solitary pursuits."[9] The result is that they may often have a feeling of "aloneness," of not being a part of the group.

Here is the statement of a sixteen-year-old gifted girl.

One day I was hurrying from one class to another when I looked around me and noticed that everyone was talking to his chum. Everyone but me! At that moment I couldn't think of a single comforting thought . . . Whenever I got that lonesome feeling I would bury myself in a book until the feeling passed, or at least until I thought it had passed. However the idea of being unwanted pursued me. . . .[10]

No amount of intellectual ability can take the place of being able to live and work and play with others.

It may sound strange to say that the gifted may feel inferior but this very often may be the case. These very

8 Story found in Witty, *op. cit.*, p. 23.
9 Strang in American Association for Gifted Children, *op. cit.*, pp. 140-1.
10 *Ibid.*, p. 139.

things of which we have been speaking may make the gifted young person feel he is different and, for the adolescent, there can be no greater evil. The gifted, too, needs affection, acceptance, and understanding. His superior abilities may separate him from others, make him feel different and, because he feels different, he feels inferior. The "feeling" of inferiority may not be related to actual ability at all and it is the feeling that counts.

The gifted child is often accelerated in school, which has definite advantages academically but it may create problems socially. Because he is younger, he often cannot compete in sports and is not accepted by members of the opposite sex or included in their social groups. Academically he may be more than their equal; socially he may feel inferior. Here is the statement of another youth of sixteen, this one a boy,

Very often I feel uncertain and unsure of myself. I know I have very little self-confidence and this has handicapped me in several ways. Even now in high school I am afraid to go over and talk to a group of girls I do not know very well because I am afraid I am not wanted.[11]

Another problem the gifted child may have is exploitation. The school, the parents, the church may overemphasize his talents. They may "show off" the young person in order to satisfy their own pride more than to develop the abilities of the child. Such children are constantly pushed and praised until they get a false picture of themselves and are alienated from their fellows.

What Are Their Assets?

The listing of these problems is not meant to give the impression that the gifted have more problems than the

11 *Ibid.*, p. 138.

average; in fact, the opposite may be true. All the studies, like those of Terman's and Hollingworth's, agree that gifted youth are superior to the general population in emotional maturity, the number of behavior problems, the incidence of delinquency, and character traits. There are exceptions, to be sure, but in the main this is true. Their giftedness does create some problems that are different but it also gives them insights which enable them to see their own situation more clearly and to find solutions more readily than others might. They can be helped to understand their own problems, to accept their own feelings, to gain acceptable goals, to develop an understanding of other people and find lives of satisfaction and usefulness.

Chapter IV

Training Gifted Youth:
The Religious Education of the Gifted

The purposes of religious education for the gifted are essentially the same as they are for everyone else. The objectives of religious education have been very adequately discussed in a number of volumes and need not be repeated here.[1] Nor are we going to present arguments for the importance of religious education. That also has been done elsewhere. This book is written with the conviction that all children need religious training. They all need an understanding of their Christian heritage. They all need the guidance and strength that come with religious knowledge and religious faith. Education that does not include religious education is incomplete; it is not adequate to meet the needs of life. As William Clayton Bower has said, "Education is an affair of the whole person in relation to his total world of reality. No education that neglects the religious adjustment of persons or the religious aspects of culture past or present can on any account be considered adequate."[2] In a day that is marked by the decreasing influence of the home, and in a country in which religion is excluded from the public schools, a definite responsibility

[1] For a discussion of the purposes and objectives of religious education, see such books as Lotz, Editor, *Orientation in Religious Education,* Abingdon-Cokesbury, 1950; or the writings of such men as William Clayton Bower, Ernest J. Chave, Harrison S. Elliott, Nevin C. Harner, and Paul Vieth. Although they do not discuss the religious education of the gifted, they do give a good presentation of the general purposes and principles of religious education.

[2] Bower, *Christ and Christian Education,* Abingdon-Cokesbury, 1943, p. 101.

is placed upon the church and the church school. If these brilliant youngsters in our communities secure religious training and guidance, it will be because the church has recognized its opportunity—no one else will do it.

Why not simply refer to the texts on religious education? Is there anything different in the religious education of the gifted from the religious education of the average? Are there any different techniques or procedures that should be used? Are the gifted young people themselves any different in their attitudes toward religion? The answer to the first question is that the texts on religious education do not give any discussion of the religious education of the gifted. The answers to some of these other questions have not as yet been given. Public education gives some helpful suggestions as to teaching techniques and procedures. There are many areas in which further investigations need to be made.

Several studies have shown that gifted children show a greater degree of interest in religion than do others and that this interest appears much earlier.[3] The gifted child is quite likely to have an intense curiosity about the meaning of the world, about the purpose of life and the reason for things. Young Pascal wanted to know the reason for everything and was never satisfied until he found satisfactory answers. When Goethe was only six years of age, he made discerning comments about sermons he heard that would do justice to an adult. When Schweitzer was just a boy, he was concerned over the fact that another boy did not have "broth twice a week" as he did and was not as strong as he was. It was a real moral question in his mind and he gave it much thought.

[3] Cf. Garrison, *Psychology of Exceptional Children*, Ronald, revised ed. 1950. p. 216ff.

Leta Hollingworth, in her study of gifted children, noted that questions of right and wrong, questions about religious matters and the meaning of life come much earlier. She disagreed with those psychologists of her day who were saying that puberty was the time when religious questions arose. She contended it was not a matter of pubescence as much as it was of mental age. When a child reached a Mental Age of about twelve, then these questions arose, she found. For a child of average mental ability, this would come at about twelve years of age, or the period of puberty, but for a child of unusual ability an MA of twelve would be obtained much earlier. In her own words, "The higher the IQ the earlier does the pressing need for an explanation of the universe occur; the sooner the demand for a concept of the origin and destiny of the self appear."[4]

Ruth Strang expresses the same thought, emphasizing the importance of helping gifted children find adequate answers and solutions to these questions. "Gifted children become concerned very early with the problems of religion and a philosophy of life. Insofar as a religious orientation to life contributes to mental health, it should be fostered in the education of gifted children."[5]

Religious education is important because of the close relationship between religion and character. Desirable moral traits seem to be correlated with high intelligence, but not always. There have been cases in history in which shrewd minds were not used for good ends. All men need character, integrity, dependability, sincerity. This is especially true of those with great capacity for good or ill. Much emphasis is being made on the need for leadership today.

[4] Hollingworth, *Children Above 180 IQ, Stanford-Binet*, World Book Company, 1942, p. 6.
[5] American Association of Gifted Children, *op. cit.*, p. 130.

It is constantly being stressed that those who are capable need to be found and trained for leadership—in business, science, statesmanship, and other areas—all of which is true. The training which they need is more than in certain skills, however; it is training in character, in an understanding of others and in a sense of social responsibility. This is a task of the church. The church is not the only agency concerned, but the church certainly should be particularly concerned.

The gifted need to be guided toward a philosophy of service for others. They need to recognize that those who have a great capacity for achievement also have a corresponding responsibility to contribute to the welfare of all. "To whom much is given, of him will much be required." Whether great capacity becomes great achievement is one of the basic questions in the life of every gifted youth. This depends on motivation, and motivation is one of the prime responsibilities of the church. The church must strengthen high ideals, create vision and purpose and faith. The gifted must find a purpose to live by, one that challenges his abilities and that he sees as being supremely worth while. He must catch a vision of his place in society, his responsibility to God, and to his fellow men. Granted that in any one church there may be only one or two young people of outstanding ability—if that one may be the Edison, the Lincoln, the Schweitzer, the Luther of tomorrow, it is worth while. If a person comes in contact with only one such person in a lifetime *and* can help him gain a Christian philosophy of life, can help him find a Christian purpose, he may be making a contribution far beyond that which he could do himself.

The leaders in the field of public education have given

the matter of the education of the gifted much thought. Much experimentation has been done and considerable research has been carried forth. While we cannot consider all of it, we should be familiar with some of their findings. Much of it applies to the church school as well as to the public school.

Some of these problems we have referred to in other chapters. We shall speak here primarily of curriculum and teaching methods. Democratic education was founded on the principle of equality of opportunity. This is good but, in practice, it has often resulted in identical opportunity. The same materials and the same methods are used with all pupils. The materials and methods that may prove of interest to the slow or average learner may be frightfully dull to the gifted child. Speaking of the curriculum, Terman said of his subjects, "It is a conservative estimate that more than half of the children with IQ's of 135 or above had already mastered the school curriculum to a point two full grades beyond the one in which they were enrolled, and some of them as much as three or four grades beyond."[6] The intellectually superior child can master the same lessons both more easily and more quickly than the average child. Hollingworth, in her special classes in New York, found that some of the students required only half the time to cover the standard amount of work that was usually assigned and some required only a quarter of the time. She said, "In the ordinary elementary school situation, children of 140 IQ waste half their time; those of 170 IQ waste practically all of their time."[7] One cannot evade the question, what about these children in church school?

6 *Genetic Studies of Genius*, Vol. 4, p. 28.
7 Hollingworth, *op. cit.*, p. 258.

In the eleventh grade in Albany, New York, it was found by actual test that the "A" or superior group had an average reading age six years higher than the average for the "C" or dull group—six years difference in reading ability, yet they were of the same chronological age. Consider again chart No. 5 in the Introduction. Here are five hypothetical children, all aged ten. If one has an IQ of 67, or is in the retarded group; if another is classified as a slow learner with an IQ of 83; if one is just average with an IQ of 100; if one is above average with an IQ of 117, and one is gifted with an IQ of 133, there is a Mental Age span of almost seven years, as is indicated by the following figures:

Chronological Age	Intelligence Quotient	Mental Age
10	67 (retarded)	6 yr. 8 mo.
10	83 (slow learner)	8 yr. 4 mo.
10	100 (average)	10 yr.
10	117 (rapid learner)	11 yr. 8 mo.
10	133 (gifted)	13 yr. 4 mo.

Yet they may all be in the same class, studying the same material.

The curriculum that fails to challenge superior abilities and to provide for individual interests sets the stage for other problems—misbehavior, boredom, and dissatisfaction with the educational experience. These are not only problems of the public school; they are problems of the church school as well.

The public school has tried to meet this problem by various methods. The three most common are acceleration, grouping, and enrichment. Each of these has advantages and disadvantages. It has been found that gifted children who are accelerated to the point at which the work is demanding are less likely to develop poor study habits or to create behavior problems than those who are held back with their own classmates. At the same time some who are accelerated too rapidly develop physical and social mal- adjustments because of the fact that they are placed with others who are older chronologically and more mature physically and emotionally. They can compete with the others intellectually but cannot participate in some athletic and social events that mean much in the life of an adoles- cent. The minister or director of religious education does not make the decision as to who is accelerated in the public school, but he should know what happens to the young person who does have such an experience.

A second method is that of grouping or separating the gifted into classes in which they can have special teachers and special curriculums. Various plans have been followed. Some schools separate the gifted only part of the time. They meet with their regular classes for part of the ses- sions and then are separated into special workshops or projects for the remainder of the day. Some schools carry on a program of released time, in which superior and gifted students are permitted to be released from their regular work for one hour or so a day for special study and training. Some provide extracurricular activities or Saturday classes which are available to those with unusual abilities in such areas as music or the arts.

Some school systems have created full-time special classes, or Major Work Classes, as they are called in Cleveland, where children are selected on the basis of intelligence and physical and social traits. Each class covers the regular curriculum but, since less time is required, many other activities and experiences can be included. This began in Cleveland with 20 students in 1922, and now has grown until, in 1956, there were 38 elementary classes, 18 junior high sections, and 13 senior high sections, with more than 1,600 students in all.[8] Other cities have instituted similar programs. Other places, like the Hunter College Elementary School in New York City, have programs in which an entire school is maintained for children of exceptional ability. Acceleration is not practiced but the emphasis is placed on enlarged training and opportunity.[9]

The third method is that of enrichment. This is an attempt through special activities, extra assignments, trips and excursions, special projects, individual reading, workshops, special interest clubs, and so forth, not merely to consume the time of the gifted child but to provide opportunities for him to pursue his interests and develop his abilities beyond that which is provided by the regular curriculum. It enables him to secure additional educational experiences other than the regular classroom activity that the average child does not have either the time or the ability to handle.

In the first of these procedures the church school is dependent upon the public school. If the public school advances a child, the church school, almost of necessity, must advance him also. If the public school does not do so, the church would find it difficult, for the simple reason that it would be difficult and probably unwise for the church school to attempt to place a child in a different grade, with

[8] Cf. Theodore Hall, *Gifted Children: The Cleveland Story*, World Book Publishing Co., 1956.
[9] Cf. Scheifele, *op. cit.*, p. 39.

pupils who are different from those he is accustomed to meeting through the week.

Grouping is impractical, at least for a vast majority of church schools. They do not have the students, the staff, or the facilities for special groups. However, it would be very helpful if the church school teacher or youth sponsor could know which ones are placed in superior groups in the public school.

The one thing the church school can adopt to good advantage is enrichment. All studies have shown the unusual interest in reading that is characteristic of the gifted. Gifted young people are often interested in biography. The lives of such personalities as David Livingstone, Phillips Brooks, Jane Addams, and Albert Schweitzer, placed in the hands of a young person, can have many values. They are interesting, first of all, and then they introduce him to an area of reading with which he may be unfamiliar. They provide much information for the experiences of such people are very much a part of our religious heritage. They present religion in a very practical and realistic way. The young person sees how his own questions and struggles were also faced in these lives and how they were worked through to a solution. He sees religion at its best, expressed in a great personality. Such stories are inspirational; they may lead to a life of commitment and service. It was the reading of the lives of Jefferson and Washington that had such a profound effect upon young Abraham Lincoln.

They are also interested in other kinds of reading such as books that interpret the value of religion and the meaning of life. A very bright girl of twelve and one-half years was given a copy of *Better Ways of Growing Up,* by Luther E. Woodward and John R. Crawford. She was bored by general classroom instruction but she was interested in understanding herself and coming to some decisions about her own educational and vocational future. This book challenged her as classroom discussion had not. Although this book is usually read by young people of 16 to 18, she read it with great care and real appreciation. She particularly enjoyed the chapters on "Light on Life's Mysteries," and "Faith to Live By." The reading of this book probably had more value than the many class sessions, the contents of which may have been of value to others but were so easy for her to grasp that they presented no challenge.

An inexpensive church library can be a real resource for such reading. It is not enough to say, "There are good books in the public library. I think you would enjoy them." When they are readily available and can be picked up and looked at, young people will often express a desire to read them. A seminary student was teaching a young people's class in a church in western New York. He made it a practice to bring several books in the area in which he was teaching and to place them on a table. Several of the more intellectually curious picked them up and took them home to read. The regrettable thing is that so much good material is available but many of the gifted young people do not even know it exists.

This desire to read can also be used to enrich the class by having a gifted young person do some special reading and report on it to the class. This should be done with great care so that it does not call attention to the greater ability of the gifted in an unfavorable way. When special reading is assigned, others should also be given special projects. Then it should be pointed out that one has one project because he likes to read; another has another project because he has interests in another area.

Many of the enrichment activities of the public school can be adapted to the church school, such as taking trips or excursions to places of special interest, planning posters or displays, making special studies, and helping with other activities.

As much as possible, enrichment activities should be related to the general activities, but in any church program there are opportunities for service projects or chances for a young person to use real creative abilities in a variety of fields, such as music, drama, public speaking, organization, and the planning and conducting of programs for other groups in the church.

The encouraging thing, as Dr. D. A. Worcester says, is that "enrichment may be provided in any class anywhere. There is no school so small, no community so isolated, that opportunities do not exist."[10] This was written of the public school but it is equally true in the church school.

It must be remembered, as he points out, that enrichment is not busy work and that what is enriching for one may be boring for another. The use of enrichment materials can be carried out in such a way that it embarrasses the individual and separates him from the group. For this reason, enrichment requires special guidance. It requires a teacher or a pastor who is willing to give the time to an individual, to attempt to understand his needs and interests, to explore with him the possibilities and resources that are available. A program of enrichment presents the teacher with both an opportunity and a responsibility. The teacher

10 Worcester, *op. cit.*, p. 40.

must be willing to give time and energy beyond the preparation of a lesson or a program for a group. He, or she, must be willing to learn and grow with the student. This, of course, is the opportunity, together with the privilege of contributing to the growth of one who may be able to make a far greater contribution than anyone else in the class or the teacher herself.

A program of enrichment may be provided for only one child in a small community, but this may have tremendous consequences. For example, some years ago, in the little village of Postville, Iowa, the pastor of a small church befriended a boy in his congregation by the name of John Mott. He recognized him as a boy of ability; he became interested in his future; he invited him to his study to talk. "He not only stimulated in him a passion for books, but guided his reading. With rare tact and sympathy and an informal way he fostered the boy's religious life."[11] He created in young Mott a desire to go on to college to continue his education, something that was unusual in a small town in that day. He had no way of knowing that this young boy would become John R. Mott, winner of the Nobel Peace Prize, President of the World Council of Churches, and leader of student groups on every continent. This does not mean to say that this pastor's efforts were the only influence that contributed to the career of John R. Mott, but they were one influence, and who knows how much different the story might have been had he not sensed his opportunity?

Whatever method, procedure, or curriculum is used, it is the teacher that is all-important. Some people say that the gifted do not need good teachers for they have a capac-

[11] Mathews, *John R. Mott: World Citizen*, Harper and Brothers, 1934, p. 15.

ity for self-teaching; they have their own incentive to learn. Nothing could be farther from the truth. Granted that they do have a capacity for self-education, the fact remains that the level of learning that is attained is determined to a large extent by the quality of the teaching. Teachers at times are jealous of the gifted. They resent the fact that they can ask questions they themselves cannot answer. A poorly adjusted teacher may be annoyed by a child's brilliance and be afraid of having him in her class. The gifted child's insights, his tendency to raise difficult issues is a threat to the teacher's security. Some consider the gifted children a nuisance for they are constantly raising their hands or raising issues unrelated to the general discussion. Some teachers ignore or suppress the gifted child's participation—all of which emphasizes the importance of the teacher in any program of education, whether sponsored by the state or by the church.

It is not uncommon in adolescence for the young person's intellectual interests and abilities to surpass those of the teacher. This is true in both the public school and the church school. Does this mean that the teacher has to be unusually brilliant, too? No. If it did, we might have a greater difficulty than we have now in staffing our church schools. It does mean that the teacher of the gifted should possess certain attitudes. Leta Hollingworth used to maintain that one prerequisite for anyone who would teach the gifted was the ability to realize that the gifted student often has more information and deeper insights into a subject than the teacher has. The teacher of the gifted needs to realize that he has not lost face if he doesn't know all the answers. Of course, the teacher of a church school class will have many questions raised that she can't answer.

This is probably true whether there are any gifted youngsters in the group or not, but when gifted children are present it is almost inevitable. Questions are the teacher's greatest opportunity. This is the growing edge of the child's mind. A child's questions may be much more important than the lesson material. When a question cannot be answered adequately, then the teacher must take the position of learning *with* the pupil and helping him as they both seek the answer together. On occasion a church school teacher may want to make arrangements for the pastor to meet with an individual pupil and help him on his quest. When such a possibility presents itself, the pastor should find time to do it, but this is the subject of the next chapter.

What, then, are the qualities of one who would teach the gifted? They are the same as for those who would teach anyone else: above-average intelligence, a knowledge of the subject matter, the ability to use certain teaching skills, to be able to lead a discussion, and so forth. To these we would add certain attitudes such as we have mentioned above: a freedom from jealousy and resentment, a reasonable amount of security, the ability to recognize individual differences, and the vision to see the potentialities in each child.

With such attitudes teachers have been able to help in the development of some who went far beyond their own capacities. One thinks of the church school teacher of John Henry Jowett, for example. Jowett testified to the influence on his life of this humble man who never achieved any fame or recognition but who made a lasting impression on the life of Jowett as a young man and was a major influence in his decision to enter the ministry. Jowett was a man of five talents; his teacher had only one or two, but he made a great contribution to Jowett's life. Consider how the influence of that pastor in a small-town church in Iowa was multiplied many times through the tremendous career of John R. Mott.

A publication of Teachers College, Columbia University, states,

The teacher holds the fate of the gifted child in her hands. She must utilize all of the resources at her command (including her own personality and teaching skill) to enrich his experience and help him grow toward complete self-realization. Her responsibility is awesome. If she fulfils it, she contributes richly to the progress of man and civilization.[12]

Such statements as this point out the tremendous opportunity that confronts the church, the church school teacher, and the pastor. The church and those interested in religious education have done little about it as yet. Before we are too critical of the church and its program of religious education, we should realize that the public school also has a long way to go. Those we have been quoting in these pages are the leaders, those who are experimenting and doing research. This has not found its way into the programs of all the schools. All educators have not been influenced by the scientific studies of the gifted. Some are plainly indifferent. All school systems would probably agree in principle that the purpose of education is to provide for the maximum development of every child in terms of his own unique possibilities, but most schools are geared to the needs of the average children (and we would in no wise minimize the importance of this) and the gifted are often overlooked and neglected. A study of 288 schools,

12 Scheifele, *op. cit.*, p. 82.

made in 1950, revealed that only two per cent reported special classes. Only nine per cent reported enrichment programs. The remaining eighty-nine per cent reported no special provision for the gifted.[13]

Before being too critical we must remember that the schools face some very real and practical problems. The rapid growth of population, coupled with the shortage of teachers, makes the mere maintaining of a regular program difficult, to say nothing of providing special opportunities for some. The typical city school situation finds the physical facilities crowded beyond capacity and the teacher loaded beyond what would be considered a normal load in the classroom. The result is that the gifted child is often lost in the melee of huge classes and large enrollments. At the same time, it is estimated that at least fifty per cent of the gifted children live in small communities or rural areas in which it is difficult to make special provisions for those with unusual talents. Such statements can give the impression that the schools are not doing much about the problem, and with that some of our leading educators would agree. Nevertheless, the schools are aware of the problem; many are thinking about it, talking about it, studying and experimenting with it. It is hoped that this volume will help to make the church aware of the situation, too.

It is not only the problem of the schools; it is the church's responsibility as well. All authorities agree that the school cannot do it alone. The school must provide for the wide range of activities needed for the gifted child. The whole community has a responsibility here and the church is a part of the community. The school cannot, and does not,

13 Passow, Goldberg, Tannenbaum, French, *op. cit.,* p. 5.

pretend to provide for the spiritual needs of these superior students. That is the church's great privilege, its reason for being.

It is not only the church school that educates. The entire church has a part to play—the service of worship, the pastor's sermon, projects of service, summer camps and conferences; all the activities of the church can have an influence on the lives of talented youth.

Chapter V

Helping Gifted Youth: The Guidance of the Gifted

Guidance has been defined as the "process of aiding individuals in making their choices, plans, and adjustments, in undertaking effective self-direction, and in meeting problems of personal living. . . ."[1] When one considers the words that are included in this definition he realizes that to help a person with his "choices," "plans," and "adjustments," to attain "self-direction," and to meet the "problems of personal living" includes practically all of the most important aspects of life. Another more informal definition describes guidance as "personal help given by someone" that is designed

to assist a person to decide where he wants to go, what he wants to do, or how he can best accomplish his purpose; it assists him to solve problems that arise in life. It does not solve problems for the individual but helps him to solve them. The focus of guidance is the individual, . . . its purpose is to promote the growth of the individual in self-direction.[2]

According to this definition guidance is any form of personal help that assists a person to grow and develop. It includes counseling, but it is more than counseling. It helps in the solving of problems; in fact, this is one of its most important aspects, but it is not limited to the solving of problems. It also includes assisting the individual in

[1] Mathewson, *Guidance Policy and Practice.* Harper and Brothers, 1949, p. 120.
[2] By permission from *Principles of Guidance*, by Arthur J. Jones. Copyright 1945. McGraw-Hill Book Company, Inc.

creating goals and objectives, in developing plans, in attaining his fullest growth and achievement. Enrichment, which we discussed in the last chapter, requires individual guidance if it is to be effective. We are not attempting to cover the entire field of guidance; we are thinking in terms of the guidance that can be provided by the pastor and religious worker (lay or professional) for gifted children and youth.

Religious Guidance

Religious guidance is the pastor's specialty. This consists of two areas: one is the solving of religious problems; the second is the fostering of religious growth. All young people have religious problems at some time or other. The gifted are likely to have them much earlier than others. We discussed that in an earlier chapter. Leta Hollingworth found not only that gifted children had a precocious concern about such matters but, because of their youth, they found difficulty in securing help. These problems may be very real to the child or young person and may be accompanied by a great deal of anxiety and sometimes a feeling of guilt. Because they are so young, few people realize they have such problems in their minds at all, and when they do raise such questions, adults often minimize or discount their importance. As a result, they are often forced to face the problem alone. William Ellery Channing went through a very difficult intellectual religious conflict during which he wrote to his uncle, "I cannot find a friend with whom I can converse on religious subjects. I am obliged to confine my feelings to my own bosom."[3] Unfortunately this describes the experience of all too many young people today.

[3] Quoted in Sweet, *Leaders of Christian Thought*, Henry Holt, 1937, p. 280.

The report of New York University's Counseling Center for Gifted Children emphasizes the problems of the gifted child at this point. It says,

In this struggle we witness the peculiar spiritual travail of highly gifted adolescents. School and community afford them little understanding and emotional support. Too frequently they fail to achieve any fundamental security within the values of their culture, and feel aliens among their fellows.[4]

They did not mention the church or the pastor as a possible source of help; actually he should be the greatest resource. Here is one of his major responsibilities.

Sometimes these religious difficulties do not present themselves until the student reaches university. It is commonly recognized that religious problems are often accentuated on a college campus. Some students are faced with the necessity of completely reorienting their thinking. Here they must reconcile their Christian faith with all of the findings of science, anthropology, sociology, psychology, history, philosophy—the whole range of modern thought. In many cases it may be the student's first contact with points of view other than his own. It may be the first time he has heard the position of his home church and that of his parents challenged. It may be further complicated by the fact that his previous religious experience may have given him a very limited religious background and training. "The scanty deposit of ideas from childhood training is insufficient capital for the intellectual market of the campus."[5]

These problems may be of an infinite variety. They may

[4] Zorbaugh, Boardman, and Sheldon, in American Association for Gifted Children, *op. cit.*, p. 104.
[5] Merriam, *Religious Counseling of College Students*, American Council on Education, 1943, p. 40.

be questions about belief in God, the Bible, the church, prayer, the teachings of Jesus, immortality, right and wrong —the list is endless. It may be a question about the relation of science and religion, the seeming ineffectiveness of the church, or the application of religion to some social issue. Thornton W. Merriam points out that there are two main types or areas of religious adjustment problems. The first concerns the relationship of the individual to some aspect of his culture, that is, his relationship to the institution of the church, to observances, Scriptures, teachings, moral codes, those things that are sponsored by churches and religious leaders. The second involves the "ultimate loyalties of the individual's life, on which the personality is, or ought to be, structured." Here the "focus is more definitely personal . . . it involves issues concerning the ultimate loyalties which ought to command the devotion of the individual."[6] Many gifted young people work out such matters independently. Others need help. Sometimes these religious problems are quite simple and can be cleared up by giving the required information. This may be done in an interview, by providing the young person with the proper books, or better, by leading him through a period of directed reading. Sometimes the problem may be very complex, highly charged with emotion, and mixed with other problems, such as the relationship with one's family, for example. Whatever the nature of the problem it is the church's responsibility. There are many people in our communities offering educational, vocational, and personal guidance to youth; most of them do not want to go into such areas as we have mentioned here. As Merriam says, "It is the churches . . . among all the institutions of society

[6] *Ibid.*, p. 4.

which persistently are concerned with the problem of ultimate meanings and loyalties and which convey from generation to generation the result of man's attempts to find a
satisfactory answer."[7]

One may raise the question, "But who is competent for
such guidance? Who can answer all the questions of even
the average youth, let alone the gifted? Who can claim to
be an authority in theology, the philosophy of religion,
the psychology of religion, church history, the Bible, and
any one of a dozen other areas where questions might arise?
The answer, of course, is that no one can be a specialist in
all of these fields. It does point up the need of thorough
and broad training on the part of the religious worker,
but no one can be expected to have all the answers. Rather
he should provide reassurance that there is nothing wrong
in raising questions, that many others have faced the same
problems. He should provide what information he can,
make the young person aware of all the resources that are
available, and then give him the feeling that there is one
who will share with him in the quest for a meaningful
faith.

Not all of religious guidance has to do with problems;
it is also concerned about spiritual development and
growth. There is an interesting trend among those in the
field of general counseling that stresses the fact that counseling is concerned not merely with the solving of problems
but with the development of all youth. Until recently those
in the field of counseling and guidance have given major
attention to the maladjusted, the failing, the delinquent.
They have conceived of their task as a therapeutic one, all
of which is good and needs to be continued. There is a

7 *Ibid.*, p. 4.

new emphasis which points out that counseling has much to offer the student with no particular problem but who has great possibilities for development. Francis P. Robinson points out that counseling should be more than clearing up problems, as important as that is; it should also lead to a higher level of conduct for all persons. He includes a chapter entitled "Higher-level Skills of Adjustment." By this he means those skills that "enable individuals not only to adjust better to frustrating situations but, more important, to attain more creative and constructive levels of behavior."[8] This emphasis is quite new in the field of general counseling, but it is old in the tradition of the church. The church has always been concerned about "higher level skills of adjustment." Such things as prayer, worship, and service to others are among its primary emphases. These things will become real for gifted children only if personal attention is given that will take into account their greater capacity and understanding. The illustration in the previous chapter of the way in which one pastor guided the development of John R. Mott is a good example. Not to help them at this point is to deprive these gifted young people of attaining their top levels of achievement and of realizing some of the deepest experiences of life.

Personal Guidance

Probably the most common form of counseling is in the field of what might be termed personal and emotional problems. These are of an infinite variety; they may consist of worry, discouragement, social adjustment, a feeling of inferiority—any one of a multitude of things. Each one

[8] Robinson, *Principles and Procedures in Student Counseling,* Harper and Brothers, 1950, pp. 19-20.

is different; each one is unique. The gifted have them as
well as the average or the retarded. Intelligence is a great
gift but intelligence does not determine whether or not a
person will be happy, or even whether he will be successful. As one gifted child said, "Unfortunately studies aren't
a very good substitute for friends." Those who would offer
guidance to the gifted must remember, as we said earlier,
that their basic needs are essentially the same as those of
anyone else, and when they are denied satisfaction, problems result. While the research studies do show that the
gifted as a group have a higher degree of adjustment, these
are figures that apply to the group as a whole and, in terms
of guidance, the gifted must be seen as individuals. Sometimes these problems are disguised for a long time and
come up unexpectedly. A brilliant young man in a student
group seemed to be the picture of confidence. He obviously
excelled others in the discussion in the church fellowship.
He had an excellent academic record. One day he sat in
the university pastor's office and said, quite unexpectedly,
"Why don't people like me?" It proved to be a very real
and serious problem. The mentally gifted child who has
not learned to get along with others, who is emotionally
immature, who feels inadequate has just as real a problem
as does the dull child. Although it is true that the intelligence of the gifted gives them a greater degree of insight
which helps them to solve problems, it also may give them
a greater sensitivity that makes them feel problems more
deeply than others. All of the principles of good counseling procedure that have been outlined in several books
must be applied here, and it must be remembered that
the gifted do have high capacity for insight and self-direction.

Educational Guidance

Educational guidance is primarily a function of the school, which is as it should be. On occasion, however, because of a good relationship that has been established, a young person will discuss his educational problems with his pastor or youth group sponsor. Education is one of the most important aspects of a young person's life. The pastor should not attempt to take the place of the school counselor, or try to do what others can do better, but if the young person comes to him he cannot push him off by saying, "That's the school's problem." His informal friendly relationship may be what the student needs most as he faces some discouraging situation or some question that may be puzzling him.

One of the real misfortunes among gifted youth is that such a high percentage of them do not secure the academic training of which they are capable and which would fit them for wider areas of service. This may be due to lack of motivation, to a limitation of funds, to family indifference, or to other reasons. The pastor is in a good position to encourage the gifted youth, to interpret the possibilities to his family, perhaps to check into scholarship resources.

Even the gifted may experience difficulty in school. In Terman's study he found a small percentage with high ability who failed academically. Occasionally this was because of physical illness or social maladjustment; most frequently it was because of poor study habits—the ease with which they had been able to do the work in high school did not prepare them for the competition of the campus. Whenever such difficulties occur, there is a loss of confidence, a feeling of failure. At such times these people need a friend who understands, who will help them through this experience and guide and encourage them to find the plan and to make the effort whereby they can get the training and education that their true abilities warrant.

Vocational Guidance

Vocational problems of the gifted young person are quite different from those of the retarded. With the retarded it is the question of finding something that he can do. With the gifted it is a problem of selecting one thing out of many possibilities that he wants to do, something that challenges his capacities. The young person of superior intelligence has so many interests and there are so many things he is capable of doing well that he finds it difficult to select one and to make preparation for it. For this reason it is felt that the gifted should not hurry their vocational choices. They should be cautioned about making premature decisions about advanced study or the choice of a lifework, but should be encourgaed to explore a wide variety of possibilities before limiting themselves to one field of specialization.

The difficulty of getting a job that enables them to use their high intelligence is another problem of the gifted. Tests given to men in the Army and Navy indicated that many of them were not in occupations requiring the full utilization of their abilities at all.[9] This leads to personal dissatisfaction and to a tragic loss to society. Girls have a greater problem than boys because of the fact that many fields are closed to them or, if not closed, the weight of tradition works against them. Many are working as secre-

[9] Cf. *Education of the Gifted*, Educational Policies Commission, 1950, p. 21.

taries who could be in one of the professions; however, the situation is rapidly changing.

There are some who feel that vocational guidance is for the specialist and that a pastor or layman in the field should not even attempt it. They point out that good vocational guidance depends upon the ability to determine the individual's vocational aptitudes, abilities, and interests, and a thorough knowledge of the world of work, the nature and the needs of the numerous occupational fields. It is felt that the pastor does not have the tools or the techniques for either. There is much truth in this point of view. The average pastor does not have the training to do aptitude testing and other vocational testing. His knowledge of the world of work in a technical sense is limited; yet in many communities, especially in rural areas, there are no specialists available. Even in some places where there are, if a gifted young person has confidence in his pastor and comes to him with his vocational problem, the pastor cannot refuse to discuss it. Many times a vocational problem is a part of another problem, such as a family problem or a religious problem. These are in the pastor's area of responsibility and he is forced to deal with the vocational question. There are occasions when the pastor can refer to a vocational counselor; there are others when of necessity he must deal with the situation himself. For these reasons he should be familiar with the general principles of vocational guidance. In vocational counseling the decision is always the individual's. The counselor's function is to help the individual see all possibilities so that he can make the decision that is right for him. Good vocational guidance is no longer thought of as giving advice or telling a person the field of work for which he is best suited. This is especially true in regard to the gifted. Rather it consists of helping the individual gain such an understanding both of himself and the field of vocations that he will make his own decision realistically. This is a long-term process. It involves many factors—personal, social, educational, economic, and spiritual. Personality is very complex. The field of vocations is very complex. To bring the two together is no simple process. It will not be done in one interview or by reading some literature but should be continued over a period of time and should utilize all the resources that are available.

The ministry is interested in vocational guidance for another reason. The choice of a vocation is a spiritual problem. This is something many vocational counselors overlook. The distinction between "making a life" and "making a living" is a false distinction. The way one makes a living determines to a large extent the making of the life. As Emil Brunner says, ". . . the attitude to work is ultimately a religious question." ". . . If people take their Christian faith seriously, everyone knows that his specific function in society is service for the common good."[10] This is true of all men but it is especially true of those with great talent, with great potential for service. This is an idea that general vocational guidance so frequently overlooks. Hoover Rupert says,

In a world gone secularly mad we need to bring the sanity of a vocational philosophy which recognizes the potential sacredness of all useful work. In a world which worships at the shrine of business and financial success as primary factors in vocational selection, we need to sound the summons to the service motives in all vocations.[11]

10 Brunner, *Christianity and Civilization*, Part II, Scribners, 1949, pp. 66, 63.
11 In *Pastoral Care*, edited by Spann, Abingdon-Cokesbury, 1951, p. 93.

Guidance for Church Vocations

One area of vocational guidance in which the pastor is expected to render a service is with those young people who are considering one of the church vocations—the ministry, religious education, the mission field, or one of the related areas such as religious journalism, religious teaching, and so forth. Here the pastor is supposed to be the specialist. He is the one to whom the vocational counselor wants to make a referral. The general counselors do not know the field; they are not familiar with denominational differences. They do not know the seminaries and their requirements. They are not acquainted with such matters as ordination or the openings that exist. General counselors have elaborate files of occupational information but they include very little on the religious or church vocations. The pastor is the one who has this information.

The temptation of the pastor, especially when dealing with a person who is gifted, is to let his enthusiasm for recruitment overshadow his function as counselor. The need is so great, the shortage of religious workers is so acute, the competition with other professions for capable young people is so stiff that a pastor is tempted to apply pressure on behalf of the ministry. The same principle of vocational guidance applies, whether the field is the ministry or one of the other professions. The decision still must be the person's own decision. No one should be pressured into the ministry. No one should make such a decision without a full understanding of all that it involves.

Recruitment is needed. The needs of the world are moral and spiritual needs. The future of the church, of society, of our Christian heritage depends upon challenging some of our most capable young people to accept positions of leadership and responsibility. Other professions are constantly seeking out the best young people in our schools and universities. They have financial inducements far beyond anything the church can offer. This is difficult competition to meet. Recruitment must always keep in mind the guidance point of view, but the needs of the church, the needs of the world, the opportunity to serve both individuals and society should be presented to gifted young people in as real and challenging a way as possible.

The Parents of the Gifted

The pastor may not always deal directly with the child. Sometimes the most effective help he can give the child is to help the parents. Parents often have been influenced by stereotyped ideas and may be somewhat concerned if they discover that a child is gifted. "I want my children to be just good, average children," is a statement heard quite often. It indicates the fear that he will have difficulty making friends, that he will be considered a bit queer if he is found to be above average. Some, fortunately only a few, are jealous of their children's superior abilities; some may resent or even minimize their exceptional talents.

Many parents are indifferent to their children's giftedness. They may not have the background to understand either their nature or their need for stimulation. Highly gifted children of parents who may have a limited educational or financial background may face a real problem in gaining the personal experiences or educational opportunities they need. This does not mean that the parents lack affection; they may not even be aware of the child's gifts or his possibilities. They do not realize his need for

experiences that develop and use his talents or that provide
an outlet for his abilities.

There are occasions when parents may go to the other
extreme; they may exploit the child, become overanxious
and overprotective and deny him the normal experiences
that are the right of every child. Parents need help in providing the child a balance between experiences that challenge his intellectual abilities and the normal socializing
activities of his own age level. In most respects they are
"just like other kids," only with greater intellectual abilities.

Gifted children have the normal conflicts with their
parents that all young people have. Here's the way one
gifted boy put it,

During adolescence, one's whole outlook on life changes. He
sees things with his own eyes and not through the eyes of his
parents. He must judge people and the world by his own
standards. At this point he has two philosophies of life we
might say; that of his parents, and his own. These two philosophies are in constant conflict until the youth can get them
straightened out in his own mind. This has been one of my
main problems. I find my own ideas in conflict with those of
my parents and this results in a disturbing situation. I want to
read different newspapers than they; they disagree with my
choice of profession. In short, I have been influenced by the
new generation growing up with me, while they seem to be
living in the past.[12]

While others may not express it so well, this is what
happens in many cases. This is a rather normal problem,
and the boy and his parents may be able to work it out by
themselves. The boy or the parents may want to talk it
over with the pastor; if so, he is in a good position to inter-

12 Quoted by Strang in Witty, *op. cit.*, p. 136.

pret each to the other. The important thing is that, in spite of such differences, the young person feels that he is secure in the affection of his parents.

When one child in a family is gifted and others are not, a possible problem is created, both for the one that is gifted and for those who are not. The one who is gifted may become conceited and looked down on others; the one who is not gifted may develop real feelings of inferiority because of the fact that he does not get as much recognition; his grades are not as high, and the constant experience of always being in second place is a difficult one. These are extremely delicate problems and may be related to others.

Whatever the problem, the pastor or youth leader needs to develop the proper attitude—not that he knows the answers but that he is searching, together with the parents, for the answers. His function is to help them understand their own situation and be aware of the resources and possibilities that are available.

Should the Gifted Know They Are Gifted?

In dealing with gifted children and their parents, should they be told that they are gifted? There are differences of opinion in this matter. Some feel that the gifted young person should not know of his superior ability because it may result in attitudes of conceit and overconfidence. On the other hand, most gifted youth are aware of their superiority, anyway. If the purpose of guidance is to help the individual to understand himself, as has been frequently stated, then he needs to take his full intellectual capacity into account, which includes his possibilities and his responsibilities. First, it should be definitely determined that the real ability is there. No opinion should be based on limited or superficial evidence. If his abilities have been carefully examined, then there is no reason why a person should not be aware of his own potential. Some young people might not have sufficient self-confidence to attempt a graduate program, for example, without such knowledge. Certainly gifted children should not be given any exaggerated notion of their own importance, and some may need to be reminded that their greater endowments do not make them any better than anyone else; rather, they give them a greater responsibility for service. If they do have unusual talent, they should be challenged to use it—for their own good as well as society's.

The Counseling Approach

Many talented young people undoubtedly would solve their problems and develop their abilities without guidance or help. Biography is filled with illustrations of this. Great ability seems to bring great insight. How many others might have emerged with the proper counseling and guidance at the right time is not known. It is not our purpose here to discuss the techniques of counseling and guidance. That has been done in many volumes. The client-centered approach to counseling is well adapted to work with the gifted. How do we know what is the best decision for this young person, vast in capacity and rich in potential? He could move in any one of a number of worth-while directions and be successful at it. Our function is to help him to help himself, to help him to understand himself and all of his possibilities. The counselor must be especially careful to listen, to let the gifted young person think through his own point of view, to encourage him to take as much responsibility as possible for his own guidance, but to feel that he can use his pastor as a resource, that he is one who understands, one who is his friend. As Dr. Witty sums it up "In order to reach the point where he can begin to guide his own life and solve his own problems, he needs our patient help and guidance, our love and understanding."[13]

13 Witty, *op. cit.*, p. 26.

Part II

The Retarded

"Truly, I say to you, as you did it to one of the least of these my brethren, you did it to me."—*Matthew 25:40.*

Chapter VI

Our Forgotten Children:
The Nature and Extent of the Problem

When we speak of the problem of the retarded child, we are not discussing some isolated matter that is the concern of a few specialists. It is a very widespread problem that concerns many people. It can occur anywhere. Mr. and Mrs. D— were typical parents. They anxiously awaited the birth of their child whom we shall call Johnny. They made great plans for his future. He was to go to college, perhaps to graduate school and into a professional career. Nothing would be spared. He seemed to be a normal happy baby, but he didn't develop as rapidly as the children of their friends. He was slow in learning to sit up and to walk; it was almost two years before he could speak. Mr. and Mrs. D— were worried and a bit frightened. They wondered what to do. They took the child to their family doctor who referred them to a specialist. They went to other doctors. Nothing seemed to help. Finally there came the realization that Johnny was a retarded child. They were confused, embarrassed, and afraid. What should they do? What of all their plans? What would their friends think? Was it their fault? Where had they been to blame? Was there anyone who could help? What should they do next?

Mr. and Mrs. D— were not the only ones concerned about Johnny. It was a real problem to the doctor when Johnny's parents brought him to the office. He wished there were more that he could do. It was not easy for him to explain the situation to Johnny's parents. A bit later, when Johnny was old enough to go to school, he presented a real problem to his teacher and to the administration, for Johnny didn't fit into the regular classroom. The school authorities didn't know just what to do either. It is a concern for government officials because many like Johnny are so retarded that they are placed in institutions. This requires funds to provide buildings, personnel, staff, care, and supervision. It should be a concern of every sensitive-minded citizen who is aware of the needs and the feelings of the unfortunate. Does not the New Testament teach us that the strong ought to bear the burdens of the weak? Did not Jesus say, "as you did it to one of the least of these my brethren, you did it to me"?

Most of all, it is a problem to Johnny himself. What happens to him when he goes out in the neighborhood to play with other children? What happens when he goes to school, when others learn to read rapidly, when others learn to write, to add, and to accomplish all the other intellectual skills? What happens when report cards are sent home? What attitudes will his family take? What happens when he appears on the playground? What happens when he has to compete in games with others who are brighter than he is? Will other children accept him? Will they welcome him into their group? What happens when he goes to church school? to church? Will he become a part of the youth group? What happens when the time comes for him to select a vocation or to try to get a job?

Is there anything Johnny's pastor can do to help? Johnny's family are members of his church. Can he do anything to relieve their feelings of guilt and frustration? Can he help them to understand and accept Johnny? Johnny, too, is a child of God. He, too, is the pastor's responsibility. What can the pastor do for him? These are some of the questions we must face here.

The story of Johnny is not an unusual one. More than 100,000 children who prove to be retarded are born each year. The number of men rejected for service in World War II proved that it is a national problem. We realize how extensive it is when we consider the statistics of the number involved. After all, half of the people in the country are below the average by the very nature of the definition. We are not speaking of any such broad, general group, however. No one knows for sure how many retarded children there are in the country. If we are speaking of the severely retarded, the figures usually quoted are from 1 to 2 per cent. One per cent does not sound too large until we consider that this means that one child out of every 100 children that are born is retarded—which means, further, that there are more than one and a half million children in the country who fall into this group. Then it takes on a much greater significance. If we take 2 per cent, that doubles it. When we consider that this equals about twice the total population of a state the size of Colorado, then it assumes even larger proportions.

These figures (1-2 per cent) do not include many borderline cases. If we add this group, our figures would double at least. It would include between 4,000,000 and 8,000,000 children. For our purposes, speaking from the standpoint of the program and responsibilities of the church, we also want to include that group that the educators refer to as "slow learners." This is a group about midway between those of average intelligence and those who would be classed as mentally subnormal or retarded. They are not severely retarded but are sufficiently below average to merit special consideration. This group is very much a part of the church and its program and should be of concern to the pastor and to the religious educator. This group would include 20-25 per cent of the public school population. By now we can see that we have quite a sizable number nationally, which includes some that are in almost every church and community.

The word "retarded" means different things to different people. It should be pointed out that there is a difference between the mentally retarded and the mentally ill. Both the mentally retarded and the mentally or emotionally disturbed children may score low on IQ tests, but it is for different reasons. There is a tendency, on the part of some people, to lump everything with the term "mental" under one heading. To speak of the retarded is to speak of a condition, not a disease.

It is also important to point out that there is a difference between the mentally retarded and the educationally retarded. The mentally retarded usually are educationally retarded. This does not mean that the educationally retarded are always mentally retarded. The fact that a child is not up to his class in performance may be because he does not have the ability; it may be because he has not had the same opportunity. A child can be educationally retarded for a variety of reasons. It may be due to the fact that the family has moved many times; it may be the result of poor health; it may be a language difficulty; it may be a lack of motivation; or it may be due to inadequate teaching. This emphasizes one basic principle. Before saying that a person is mentally retarded, we should be sure that this is what the situation really is.

There are many different terms that are used to describe

the mentally retarded. Some are used quite frequently and interchangeably. A layman in the field is quite likely to be confused by references to the feeble-minded, the mentally deficient, the mentally handicapped, the idiot, the imbecile, the moron, the slow learner, the dull normal, and the borderline. Many of these terms are technical terms and should be used as such. They have a meaning to the specialist and should not be used where they do not apply.

When we speak of the mentally retarded, in general, we are referring to those who do not have as much intellectual ability as others. In many ways, they are like other so-called normal people except that they are operating at a lower level of intelligence. Because of this fact there are certain things they cannot achieve and cannot do. With some, the level of intelligence is so low that they need continuous care and supervision. Others can live in the community, can even maintain themselves, but they have certain limitations intellectually.

According to an old statement, "The test of any civilization is the point below which the weakest and most unfortunate members are permitted to fall." Our civilization permits some to fall pretty low. Some people feel that the retarded are one of the most unfortunate groups of all. They are treated with less understanding, less respect, and greater rejection than any others. One of their greatest problems is the lack of public sympathy and understanding, including that of those who are in the churches.

Ours is a culture that worships at the shrine of success. Success is usually conceived of in terms of monetary return, intellectual achievement, or public recognition. We live in a society in which education is exalted—as it should be. Compulsory school laws, increased enrollment at our institutions of higher learning, greater requirements for most professions and vocations are commonly accepted. The retarded cannot attain success, as usually defined, either educationally or vocationally. They never experience the feeling of important accomplishment, recognition, or attainment. Their contributions to society, limited as they are, are often regarded as unimportant in our society.

Experienced workers with the retarded are constantly emphasizing the fact that they do have a contribution to make, that much can be done, both with and for them, that many have not reached their full potential because no real effort has been made to help them. They have not been understood; they have not been given the guidance or the training that they have needed. When we consider religious training, a great percentage of them have had none at all.

All of this is of importance to the church and to the pastor. The pastor, by virtue of his calling, is concerned about every individual. These people are in his community; they may be in his church school or youth group; their families are in his church. Those at the very low level are in institutions. Here also the pastor should be interested in the kind of care and training that they receive. The dull normal, the slow learner, the low average are in every community and must be dealt with directly. The pastor has a responsibility to them as well as to other children. He should know something of the general principles that have been revealed as a result of the research and experimentation that has been done that will guide him in the development of his own program and his contacts with individuals as he tries to meet their personal and spiritual needs.

The pastor has an interest in society. He is interested in social attitudes and public institutions. He is concerned about "the point below which some of society's weakest and most unfortunate members are permitted to fall." The retarded, because of his childish mind, can be and occasionally is led into difficulties by more intelligent but unscrupulous individuals.

The church has said much about the mission fields around the world and should continue to do so. Here is another mission field, right at its doorstep. If the pastor, the religious educator, the worker with youth can gain some understanding of the nature of the problem, perhaps a few frustrations and heartaches might be eased. Enough has been achieved already to know that some results can be attained. Many who are not too severely retarded have proved their ability for some forms of employment and have taken their place as respected citizens. Many retarded boys and girls have been helped to grow and develop within their own limitations. "Their cup is not as large as the normal person's, but it can be filled."[1]

Give them a chance. The Golden Rule applies to them. We are to do for them what we would others should do for us. Give them justice and a fair chance. Do not throw them into a world where the scales are weighted against them. Do not ask them to gather grapes of thorns or figs of thistles. But give them one chance to bring out the best that is in them. This is but a fair request on behalf of human beings who nevertheless are permanent children and who will never grow up. . . . The achievements of life, for them, are bounded by their mental make-up and character—just as our achievements are, though on a little larger scale.[2]

[1] *Our Forgotten Children*, National Association for Mental Health, p. 17.
[2] Helen MacMurchy in *The Almosts*.

Chapter VII

Centuries of Neglect:
The Historical Background

Pearl Buck has written, "In every age however troubled there are always heartening events. One of the most encouraging of our times is the awakening of the public to the needs and rights of the mentally retarded child."[1] Considering the history of the treatment of the retarded, it is a temptation to say, "It has been a long time coming"; but the fact remains that a new interest and concern are evident and, for that, everyone should be grateful. We can have a new appreciation and clearer perspective if we consider briefly the historical background of our present-day situation.

The history of the treatment of retarded children and youth is a rather pathetic record of mistreatment, persecution, and neglect. The story of "man's inhumanity to man" is a sad story and this is one of its most unfortunate chapters.

In ancient times the feeble-minded were often ridiculed and exploited or cast out to perish. The Spartans were said to have thrown them into the river or abandoned them on the mountainside. With the spirit of compassion that came with the Christian movement there were some groups who attempted to care for these unfortunate individuals who acted peculiarly and who could not learn like other children. The Christian teaching introduced a new spirit of

[1] Preface to Jacob, *New Hope for the Retarded,* Public Affairs Pamphlet 210, 1954.

thoughtfulness and understanding into society that would eventually result in many changes throughout the centuries, but it came very gradually and very slowly. With the exception of occasional acts of kindness, it was a long time before any general attempt was made to educate or help them.

For centuries, backward people were ridiculed, called "fools" and "idiots," and, during the medieval period, were sometimes subjected to barbaric punishment. One of the first records of merciful care was that of the Bishop of Myra (the St. Nicholas of Christmas) in the fourth century. In the seventeenth century a chateau to shelter the unfortunate, including the feeble-minded, was begun by St. Vincent de Paul. But these were isolated instances. Those who were the recipients of their kindness were fortunate, but the majority were the victims of neglect, often the laughingstock of the community. No one thought of being able to do anything for them. As one man put it,

They have come down through the ages of human development and have fitted severally into the existing order of things as best they could, and have passed away each in his turn—little lamented, no doubt, by those on whom they have been a burden, and soon forgotten by the world.[2]

No real attempt to do anything for these children in a scientific or humanitarian way was made until the nineteenth century. No extensive efforts were made to provide educational opportunities prior to 1800. During colonial days pupils who were slow in school were punished by being forced to wear a "dunce cap" and sit before the class, and thus were made to feel ashamed of their stupidity. Those who pioneered in the education of the mentally

---

[2] Peterson, *Early Conceptions and Tests of Intelligence*, World Book Co., 1925, p. 23.

defective were primarily medical men who were interested in the development of these children.

One of the first to attempt to be of service to these people was the French philosopher and physician, Jean Marc Itard. He was working in an institution for the deaf and came to the conclusion that similar methods of training might be of help in the training of the feeble-minded.[3] He is remembered because of his famous experiment with the so-called "wild boy of Aveyron." About 1799, in the forest of Aveyron, a boy about twelve years old was found. No one knew anything of his background. He was living very much like an animal and his reactions were more animal than human. He could not speak and selected his food by smell, with no apparent discrimination between foul and pleasant odors. Itard felt that the boy was a good example of one completely untaught and felt that with the proper educational procedure he could be made human. Pinel, the French psychiatrist, diagnosed him as an idiot and felt that the boy never could be educated.

Itard, nevertheless, began an extensive training program which he continued for five years. After five years he felt that the experiment was a failure and gave up the project. The French Academy of Science investigated the case, felt that what he had done was a significant contribution to learning and persuaded him to publish a report on his experiment. This he did under the title *The Wild Boy of Aveyron,* a book which many consider a classic in the history of the education of the retarded child. It was the first extensive record of the training of an idiot with any objective reports of the progress. Itard attempted to

[3] For this account see Kirk and Johnson, *Educating the Retarded Child,* Houghton Mifflin, 1951, p. 70ff.

develop the senses separately but with little success. He hoped he could create in the boy some human wants and desires but, aside from an evident fondness for Itard and the woman who cared for him, the boy paid little or no attention to other people. He never learned to speak and recognized only a few simple words when continuously associated with objects, but he never learned to read. Itard hoped that with the onset of puberty the situation would improve, but the opposite resulted. The boy became unmanageable and was sent to an institution. Itard discontinued his work with the feeble-minded and returned to his work with the deaf.

Although Itard was not successful in his efforts with the wild boy of Aveyron, his work was a stimulus that did much to promote the interest of others. One of his most noted pupils was Edward Seguin, who was challenged by the potentialities of mentally defective children and devoted his whole life to their training and treatment. His approach was termed the "physiological method," which he described in a book published in 1846, and entitled *The Moral Treatment, Hygiene, and Education of Idiots, and Other Backward Children*. With the publication of this volume he received rather wide recognition and was even crowned by the French Academy and commended by the Pope.

Later Seguin came to the United States where he became superintendent of the Pennsylvania Training School for Idiots. However, he disliked administrative work and was further handicapped by his limited knowledge of the English language, so he retired from the institution and spent twenty years in the private tutoring of retarded children in New York. In accordance with his "physiological method" of education he felt that the first task was to educate the muscular system. Activities must be those that satisfy the child's needs, desires, and capacities. He laid great stress on the importance of the training of the hand for it incorporates many related skills, both physical and mental. He felt that speech was the most difficult skill for the retarded to acquire and attempted to teach first speech, then writing, and then reading. Further elaboration of his methods and pioneer efforts need not be included here.

Many improvements have taken place since his day but some of his principles anticipated later developments. He advocated the education of the whole child, the individualization of instruction, and the importance of rapport between teacher and pupil. Seguin's religious motivation may be seen from a speech which he made at the laying of a cornerstone for one of the first buildings erected expressly for the care of the mentally retarded. He said,

"God has scattered among us—rare as the possessors of genius— the idiot, the blind, the deaf mute, in order to bind the rich to the needy, the talented to the incapable, all men to each other, by a tie of indissoluble solidarity. The old bands are dissolving; man is already unwilling to continue to contribute money or palaces for the support of the indolent nobility; but he is every day more ready to build palaces and give annuities for the indigent or infirm, the chosen friends of our Lord Jesus."[4]

There were others who pioneered in the development of some form of training for the mentally retarded. Dr. Deteressa Maria Montessori was an assistant in a psychiatric clinic in Rome where she became interested in a number of mentally deficient children. After studying the work of

[4] From *Forgotten Children*, National Association for Mental Health, p. 16.

Itard and Seguin she came to the conclusion that the problem of mental deficiency was primarily pedagogical rather than medical. Consequently she organized a school for feeble-minded children and also conducted a training school for teachers. Some of her results were so marked that she attempted the same procedures with normal children. She made a special attempt to relate home and school in the training of the child. Her work attracted wide attention and received both praise and criticism by those educators who studied it.

Dr. O. Decroly, in Brussels, was another physician who became interested in the mentally retarded. He also was convinced that the solution of the problem was an educational one and, with his workers, did much to utilize educational games and activities. In America, Dr. Samuel G. Howe, who is primarily noted for his work with the blind, started a class for the training of idiots in 1837, and was largely influential in the establishment of the Massachusetts School for Idiotic and Feeble-minded Youth.

Not all those interested in the mentally retarded were physicians. Horace Mann, after a visit to Europe in 1842, advocated special schools for the feeble-minded. In July of 1848 a private school for retarded children was established at Barre, Massachusetts. This is the oldest private institution in America. In 1851 an experimental school was opened in Albany, New York, and in 1887 a private school was opened in Millville, New Jersey. It was later moved to Vineland, New Jersey, where it became known as the Vineland Training School. This school has continued through the years and has made an excellent contribution to the whole movement. In Europe several public school systems established special classes for the retarded, the first

being at Halle, Germany, in 1859. This idea was trans-
ported to America. There is a difference of opinion as to
what city was the first to incorporate such a program but
by 1900 several had established such classes. We will discuss
this further in Chapter IX, "The Religious Education of
the Retarded."

It was because of his interest in the retarded child that
Binet developed his intelligence scale that we have described in an earlier chapter. He was commissioned to
discover a means whereby those who were unable to profit
by regular educational procedure could be recognized. In
his own words,

> The main purpose of the authors (Binet and Simon) in the
> devisal of these tests is to furnish to the teacher a first means
> by which he may single out mentally backward children, who,
> upon further examination, may also be found to have some
> mental defect or peculiarity which prevents them from fully
> profiting by the education of the ordinary school, and who
> probably would benefit more by being educated in a special
> school or in a special class.[5]

Binet did not organize or develop an educational program. His contribution was to provide a method of diagnosis whereby the mentally retarded could be recognized.

Several types of schools have been created for the training of the retarded. The movement for state schools, which
began in Massachusetts, spread very rapidly. At the present
time there are more than seventy such schools in the country with a resident population of more than 100,000. There
are two kinds of private schools, those that are individually
owned and operated, and those that have been established
by some religious or philanthropic organization. These are

[5] Binet and Simon, *Mentally Defective Children*, translated by W. B. Drummond,
N. Y., Longmans Green & Co., 1914, pp. v-vi.

usually operated by a staff that is supervised by a board of trustees or some similar body. Private schools are usually small and thus can provide opportunity for individual attention and instruction. At the present time there are more than two hundred private schools in America. Some communities have established day schools which permit the retarded child to remain at home as other children do but come to this school for special instruction. Some of these are related to the public school and some are privately owned and operated.

In spite of these facilities many children do not receive the training that they need. A great number are in their own homes and communities and receive no training at all. A bulletin of the National Association for Mental Health says that in a typical state where there are 50,000 mentally retarded, it is not likely that more than 4,000 will be in training schools and about the same number in special classes. Because of the overcrowded conditions in some of these training schools some children may be on a waiting list for months and even years.

A new resource was created in 1943 when the 78th Congress passed Public Law 173, which made available a program of vocational rehabilitation for the mentally, as well as the physically handicapped. This is a program sponsored and financed jointly by the state and federal governments. It makes available special vocational training for those retarded young people who are able to profit by vocational training. Before a person is accepted, a careful diagnostic study—medical, psychological and social—is made to determine whether or not he can benefit from such training and in what areas he is most likely to be able to achieve some degree of vocational success.

In 1950 the National Association for Retarded Children was formed. Parents of mentally retarded children began to organize as early as the 1930's because they had found that collectively they could work for their children's welfare much better than they could alone. They founded co-operative schools and similar projects and did much to support each other through shared experiences and feelings. Following the war, the movement expanded very rapidly and representatives of thirteen states met to form the National Association. It is a nonprofit, nonsectarian federation of local and state associations dedicated to promoting the welfare of all mentally retarded persons. The National Association for Retarded Children serves as a clearing house and central source of information regarding the retarded. It helps to create public awareness of the problem and to sponsor legislation that will benefit the retarded. They stimulate and sponsor scientific research and provide an advisory service for all professional groups. At the local level they sponsor clinics, nursery schools, day-care centers, and sheltered workshops. They now have more than 400 local and state units and a membership of more than 50,000 persons.[6]

In recent years there has been an increasing interest in this problem on the part of many professional groups. It has been reflected by the publication of many books and articles in both professional and popular journals that have called attention to some phase of the problem. Some rather prominent people, such as Pearl Buck and Dale Evans, have published books and articles on the subject. These have done much to stimulate public interest.

A noted professor of pediatrics made the statement,

6 National Association for Retarded Children, 99 University Place, New York 3, N.Y.

To one like myself who has been confronted and frustrated for many years as a pediatrician with some of these problems, it is heartening to observe the development during the past few years of profound and urgent concern with the subject. This concern is manifested in the ranks of many diverse groups— parents, physicians, psychologists, sociologists, scientific investigators, social workers, educators. . . .[7]

It is a bit disturbing that he did not include the ministry or the church among those who are concerned. Perhaps it was an oversight; yet we must admit that, from the brief historical sketch we have made here, the church has not played a prominent part in the movement for the welfare of the retarded.

This does not mean that the church has been without influence. It has been the spirit of Christian compassion and concern that has motivated much of that which others have done, though their efforts may not have been specifically in the name of the church or under its auspices. This is one of the greatest contributions the church can make, to keep alive this spirit of compassion that motivates and influences all professions and all areas of life. Some religious groups have established schools and homes for the retarded. Some religious bodies have provided chaplains that have served in both private and state schools. Some pastors have shown great understanding of the needs of the retarded and their families. There have been no extensive attempts to study the problem or to provide guidance for pastors in dealing with the retarded. It is an area that has been largely neglected by religious education, pastoral psychology, and theological training. It is hoped that in the future the church, together with these other areas of education—

[7] From Grover F. Powers, M. D., in the Foreword to Heiser, *Our Backward Children*, W. W. Norton, 1955, p. 11.

medicine, social work, and so forth—will play a much more prominent part in helping these children, limited in ability though they are, to understand the love of God and to find a life that is meaningful for them. It is a task in which all groups need to unite their efforts in a spirit of Christian understanding and Christian love.

Chapter VIII

Understanding Retarded Children: The Psychology of the Retarded

Any desire to help the backward or retarded child or young person should begin with an attempt to understand him. Mental retardation is incomplete mental development. It is a limitation of capacity. It is not something that can be "cured" or fundamentally changed. It is not something a child will spontaneously outgrow. With the best medical care from birth, and with proper guidance and training, however, considerable improvement can be brought about in many instances. Our purpose is to understand and thus to help.

In one sense there is no psychology of the retarded. Each one is unique—each one is different; each one has his own psychology. The mentally retarded come from every race, every nationality, every section of the country. They can be found in any part of the community.

Classification of the Retarded

There have been many attempts to classify the retarded or mentally deficient. Among the first to do so was H. H. Goddard, at Vineland. He spoke of the idiot, the imbecile, the moron, and the borderline case. These classifications have been rather widely accepted with varying interpretations. A rather common division is to speak of the idiot as having a mental age of 0 to 3 years, with an IQ range of o to 19; the imbecile, a mental age of 3 to 7 years and an IQ range of 20 to 49; and a moron, a mental age of 7 to 12 years, with an IQ range of 50 to 75.

In terms of performance an idiot is one who is so completely retarded from birth or early childhood that he is unable to care for himself, or to guard against common physical dangers. He needs constant supervision. An imbecile is one who can be taught to care for his personal needs but is too retarded to be able to care for his own affairs. He may be able to do some work under supervision but he cannot support himself. He can acquire some language but has very limited ideas. A moron, although retarded, can often get along in a community where life is simple and where demands placed upon him are not too heavy. Morons can work under supervision and many become either partially or wholly self-supporting. Their ideas are limited but they can profit from special education and training. The borderline cases are much more difficult to classify as there is greater variation and the complicating factors of motivation make it difficult to determine whether failure of performance is due to lack of ability or to lack of effort.

These terms "idiot," "imbecile," and "moron" are technical terms. They should be used by the psychologist and the professional worker with the retarded, not by the pastor or the layman in the field.[1]

1 A distinction should be made between the grossly feeble-minded and the more generally retarded or borderline cases. The latter group, the borderline or dull, follow the laws of heredity with much more frequency than does idiocy. Idiocy may occur among the highly intelligent as well as among the average or below average. There are certain causative factors that explain some of this. For example, there is an unusually high incidence of idiocy born of mothers who are ill with German measles during the first three months of pregnancy. Authorities have found that there is sometimes an inherited gene defect which turns a chemical found in ordinary food into a brain poison and may result in extreme retardation. Where this is known and a special diet is used, some significant results have been attained. It should be understood that this is something of a biological accident. It is a result of a combination of highly complicated

There is a trend away from the use of such terms at all. A pamphlet published by the National Association for Mental Health, prepared by Arnold Krause of Vineland and Grant M. Stoltzfus of the Woodbine Training School, of Woodbine, New Jersey, suggests that we replace the terms "idiot," "imbecile," and "moron" with "low grade," "middle grade," and "high grade." The range of intelligence would be essentially the same, but they feel that this makes it clearer that mental retardation is a matter of levels.[2]

Samuel Kirk and Orville Johnson, writing as educators, speak of the (1) feeble-minded, or mentally deficient, (2) the mentally handicapped, and (3) the slow learners. The first require special custody and cannot profit from education; the second are educable to some degree if given special attention; the third can participate in regular classes but have difficulty. They correspond to the borderline cases and are difficult to classify. They can pass for normal children, but they have trouble in school and seldom attend college, but are capable of vocational success in limited fields. We shall speak of them again in the next chapter but mention it here because it is one form of classification.

A handbook which was prepared for volunteer workers in the Kentucky Training Home speaks simply of "the severely retarded," the "moderately retarded," and the "mildly retarded."[3] These are perhaps good terms for the

---

biochemical factors about which no one could have known and for which no one could be blamed. In other words, in such cases there is a special causative factor which is different from that of the less severely retarded who follow the more usual lines of heredity.

[2] See *Forgotten Children*, National Association for Mental Health, pp. 9-11.

[3] Jarvis, Morgan, and Williams, *A Handbook for Volunteers with Mental Defectives*, the Kentucky Training Home, Frankfort, Ky., mimeographed.

layman to use. When one considers individual young people he will find that the categories often overlap. There are no such things as clear-cut divisions. Certainly the pastor should not attempt to classify but to understand.

Identification and Diagnosis

The identification and diagnosis of a person as being mentally retarded should always be made with great care. Such a diagnosis should be made only after a careful analysis of all clinical data, including family history, social history, school history, school experience and progress, a physical examination, including speech, vision, and hearing, a consideration of emotional and personality factors, as well as the traditional intelligence test. In other words, diagnosing mental retardation is a highly technical matter, in more difficult cases requiring the co-ordinated efforts of several specialists—pediatrician, psychologist, psychiatrist, neurologist, and educator.

It is sufficient for our purpose to make clear that the pastor is never the one to make the diagnosis. He should not even venture an opinion until others have made their examinations.

There are some forms of mental retardation that are evident from their appearance. The mongoloid and cretin can be identified because of their unusual appearance. This is not true of many others and they must be identified by other means.

Of all the methods mentioned above for diagnosing retardation, the IQ or the intelligence test is the most common. Even this should be used with caution. Tests can be wrong. A low test score on an intelligence test may be due to a lack of opportunity, to limited ability, to lack of motivation, to poor administration on the part of the tester, or to a number of other factors. For this reason a low test should always be rechecked. There have been instances in which people were committed to institutions for the retarded whose low scores were later found to be due to emotional disturbances or physical handicaps, such as hearing or vision. These are exceptions but they have happened.

Here is an actual case of a young man of thirty years of age who had been in a state school for retarded children since he was a child. Because of a speech defect and personality factors he appeared dull. Upon examination he was found to have an IQ of 114. He was trained as a printer's helper. It took some counseling to assure him that he could go out on his own. At first he left the home just in the daytime, returning at night. Later he went to a neighboring city where he was employed as a printer. This is not an isolated case. No one knows how many more such situations exist that never have been detected.

We repeat that all low scores should be checked and re-checked periodically. Improved surroundings, the elimination of emotional factors, better educational opportunities, and increased motivation may alter the situation.

Also, the IQ is not the whole story. It says nothing about social or personality patterns. Two children may have identical scores of 48 and one may be slovenly, unkempt, unco-operative and difficult to handle; the other may be neat, friendly, and well-adjusted to others.

Physical Characteristics

What are the physical characteristics of the retarded? Most of them have no distinguishing features, with the exception of the clinical types we mentioned above: the mongoloids, the hydrocephalic, the microcephalic, and the cretins.[4] This comprises about 12-15 per cent of all the retarded. Others may not have the same alertness of expression that is characteristic of the gifted child, but this is not sufficient basis for a diagnosis.

Some retarded children are healthy, some are unhealthy. The mortality rate is much higher among the retarded than among the average; this is the reason there are more retarded children than retarded adults in our communities. Advances in medical science and public health are lowering the mortality rate among retarded children all the time.

The retarded are much more likely to have physical problems and handicaps than are the average or the gifted. Some people say that physical defects are twice as frequent among the retarded as among others. Part of this may be due to the fact that their physical problems may not have received the medical care and attention they needed.

Sometimes these physical disabilities have resulted in false diagnoses of feeble-mindedness. The child who has had a severe hearing handicap from childhood, for example, has not had a normal opportunity to acquire language, to profit from conversation or teaching, or to enjoy those experiences which can be measured by intelligence tests. The problem is that sometimes these disabilities are not suspected or discovered until after a person has been classified as mentally deficient.

Personality Characteristics

A number of studies have been attempted to determine

[4] For a brief description of these characteristics, see *Forgotten Children*, National Association for Mental Health, Jacob, "New Hope for the Retarded Child," Public Affairs Pamphlet. For a more extended discussion see any standard psychology of the retarded. The mongoloids receive their name from the fact that they resemble orientals; the hydrocephalic has a large, abnormally shaped head; the microcephalic has a small head, and the cretin a dwarfed body, often a large head caused by an insufficient secretion of the thyroid gland.

the personality characteristics of the retarded child. They do not show any general pattern that is peculiar to this group. They do not reveal any reactions in this group that did not exist to some extent in other groups. Most mentally retarded children are similar to other children and, like other children, some have personality problems. All behavior is caused, and the retarded child is subject to some pressures that may result in unfortunate behavior. When he is pushed beyond his ability, when he is taunted by the group, he may react by becoming overly aggressive or he may lose all confidence and become shy and withdraw from the group.

Some of the responses of the retarded are different from those of other children. The retarded have a sense of humor; they love funny things but their sense of humor is quite different from that of the gifted child, for example. They do have limitations in personality, but they have essentially the same feelings. The statement used with reference to the gifted can be used here: like other children, they desire attention, acceptance, and affection. They like the praise and attention that come with the accomplishment of some task, but this is something they seldom receive. The sense of satisfaction and confidence that comes with accomplishment is largely denied them. The sheer joy of achievement is something they do not know.

No one likes to experience failure, and constant failure is demoralizing even to a normal person. The retarded child has experienced failure countless times. Retarded children have been placed in situations in which they are unable to accomplish by grade standards. It is not only in the matter of grades and the comparison with their classmates that they fail. They know that in the eyes of their teacher and often their parents they have failed, too. It is no wonder they often have so little self-confidence.

Present conditions all contrive to make this situation more difficult for the retarded. Compulsory and universal school laws keep them in an academic environment in which they are unable to perform as well as others. The premium placed on intelligence in our culture, the competitive requirements for jobs, the complexity of society as a whole all make it difficult for the retarded.

Ruth Strang, out of years of experience as an educator, says,

The failing student is usually a pathetic figure—lacking security, ego satisfaction, and approval. Usually he finds himself subject to the criticism of his parents, the exhortations of his teachers and harassing doubts about his abilities.[5]

Failure is his common experience, not only in school but everywhere.

The borderline case, the slow learner, is often misunderstood. He does not appear any different from anyone else his age. It is frequently thought that he is unwilling to put forth the effort to succeed, whereas he may not be able to succeed or to compete with others his age no matter how hard he tries. Even his parents may not understand the limitations of what he can do.

All of these things destroy his sense of belongingness. The retarded child (every child, for that matter; but especially the retarded child) must feel that he is a desired and accepted member of the family, the group, the school, or the church. This is more difficult for him because his sense of belongingness has been so frequently challenged by feelings of undeserved failure, by misunderstanding and the rejection of the group.

[5] Strang, *Educational Guidance: Its Principles and Practice*, Macmillan, 1948, p. 143.

Social Skills and Attitudes

One of the problems of the retarded is the development of social skills and attitudes that enable him to get along with others, that help him in gaining and in keeping employment, and that, in turn, will help him gain the sense of acceptance, security, and belonging that we mentioned above.

The difficulty is that retarded children are often isolated and rejected by their classmates and playmates. A study by two educators of the University of Illinois of the acceptance of the mentally retarded in the regular classroom showed that over 46 per cent were rejected by their classmates as compared to only a little over 4 per cent of the regular students. When the average children were interviewed to determine the cause of their rejection, they almost never mentioned a lack of learning ability but of unacceptable behavior, such as fighting, bullying, showing off, misbehaving, cheating, and so forth. Typical answers were, "He teases me"; "he pulls my hair"; "he hits me over the head with his lunch bucket"; "he says bad things"; "he steals my bicycle"; and so forth. Most of this behavior can be interpreted as compensation for a failure to achieve or gain recognition in any other way.[6]

Like the gifted child the retarded child has difficulty in communication, but for opposite reasons. The gifted child has a vocabulary so much in advance of his peer group that he is not understood. The retarded child has such a limited vocabulary that he expresses himself faultily; he has a scarcity of ideas and his statements are poorly phrased. His understanding of words is so much more limited than that

[6] Johnson and Kirk, "Are Mentally Handicapped Children Segregated in the Regular Grades?" reprint of *Journal of Exceptional Children*, Vol. 17, No. 3, Dec., 1950.

of his classmates that he cannot participate meaningfully in conversation.

The Retarded—Delinquency

Do the mentally retarded tend to be delinquent? The answer is that some do and some do not. That is true of every group. There are many young people with low IQ's who are in corrective institutions or reformatories. Some studies have shown that from 15 to 30 per cent of those in reformatories would be classified as retarded. It is also true that there are many young people with low IQ's who are not in reformatories and who have never been accused of delinquent behavior. It should be pointed out that the retarded are much easier to apprehend and are much less likely to have adequate legal counsel. Also the judges are much more likely to make other adjustments for a young person who shows intellectual promise than for a retarded child or youth.

Because they are more suggestible than average children and have less power of evaluation they are more likely to be misled by unscrupulous persons or older delinquents; and therefore it is not surprising that some of them are led, or drift, into delinquent behavior. Denied the satisfactions that other young people achieve, rejected by their own group, they often go to others who will accept them, but for unfortunate, even unscrupulous, purposes. Even so, only a small percentage of retarded children become delinquent.

Older Young People

A word should be said about the older young people in the community. Some may have been in institutions where they received manual and trade instruction and now they have returned to their communities in which they can be at least partially self-supporting. Some of them may have been in special classes in the public school where they received special attention and training; some may just have dropped out of school. Now they are expected to be responsible citizens, to compete in the social and vocational world. Like the slow-learning child mentioned above, they are often misunderstood. They are often not accepted or understood by employers, neighbors, or fellow church members. It should always be remembered that, though they must cope with the world as adults, they have only the mental capacity of a child. In many areas they cannot compete on equal terms with normal people. The pastor should not only be aware of this situation but should help others understand it also. If such people are not accepted in the fellowship of the church, where can they expect to be accepted?

Our Attitudes

All that we have said underlies the importance of our attitudes; by "our" we mean the attitudes of the pastor, the religious educator, the volunteer worker with youth, the church, the community as a whole. A statement of the National Association for Retarded Children points out that many can be cared for at home; many can find a place in society; they can make a contribution *if*, "if the community in which they live demonstrates intelligent and sympathetic understanding for their needs." The church is a part of the community in which they live. The church through the centuries has stood for a spirit of compassion and love—toward all. As the statement says, the church must be intelligent and informed. It must recognize retardation for what it is. The retarded must be accepted for what they are and treated as naturally as possible. The emphasis should not be on what they cannot do but on what they can do if they have the opportunity to develop their full potential. With acceptance, understanding, special training, and help wherever possible, many can become well-adjusted, happy, responsible members of society, making their own contribution in their own way. This is all that is expected of anyone.

Chapter IX

Training Retarded Youth: The Religious Education of the Retarded

Public education has given much more attention to the retarded child than has religious education. Those interested in public education have spent a great deal of time in experimentation and research. Much of this has been published in books and in numerous articles in educational journals. The needs of the retarded are included in most of the courses of teacher training. The church has much to learn from public education at this point.

The goals and objectives of education for the retarded child are essentially the same as they are for normal children. It is hoped that he will attain certain skills of language, reading, and writing that will enable him to get along in society. It is hoped that his educational experience will give him a certain amount of knowledge and information about the world in which he lives. It is hoped that, if possible, he will gain sufficient background to enter some trade or vocation and to become a useful member of society. Furthermore, it is hoped that his education will help him make social adjustments, to live better, to enjoy life more, and to become a responsible citizen.

The means of attaining these goals, or the degree to which they can be attained, are sometimes different. Goals for the retarded differ in nature because of the fact that the future of the retarded is different. When the retardation is severe, some of these skills cannot be attained and future vocational training or achievement cannot be expected. Some of the accomplishments required by the regular school curriculum cannot be expected of these children. Nevertheless, they have the right to develop their own capacities to the full measure of their possibilities.

Public education meets this problem by the organization of special classes or sections designed to meet the needs of retarded children. These are known as "ungraded" or "opportunity" classes and are meant to take the place of the old methods of failing a child or holding him back until he finally dropped out of school. In this way he is placed with children of his own abilities, physically, socially, and mentally, rather than being forced to compete with children who are superior to him in every respect.

Some people have objected on the grounds that such a form of segregation is undemocratic and unfair, that it may even be humiliating to the child if he discovers that he is in a "slow" group. On the other hand, the advocates of such a method point out that *"A child cannot be more cruelly segregated than to be placed in a room where his failures separate him from other children who are experiencing success."*[1] Children themselves segregate other children who are different, and nothing can be more humiliating than to be held back in a grade of younger and smaller children. Whenever possible, members of special classes should be assimilated into the general school program, but the special classes free them from the frustration of unfair and impossible competition and make available teachers who have had special training and can utilize special skills and techniques. Small communities find it difficult to include such a program but it is an accepted part of the school sys-

---

[1] National Society for the Study of Education, *op. cit.*, p. 24.

tems of practically all larger cities. Much still needs to be done before public education has solved the problem, but they are giving it increased attention.

What of religious education? As we said when we discussed the religious education of the gifted, the general purposes or objectives of religious education for the retarded are essentially the same as they are for average children. Unfortunately, there is a large percentage of our population that receive no religious education at all. This is true of the average and the gifted as well as the retarded. Of all groups, however, the retarded probably have the highest percentage that are neglected, that are overlooked, that are not included in any program of any sort.

There are problems related to the religious education of the retarded. They do have intellectual limitations. They cannot keep up with other children in comprehension and understanding. The public school meets this by segregation and special classes. The church school does not have either the staff or the facilities for such a procedure.

Those who work with the retarded all of the time, like Walter Jacob, director of the training school at Vineland, New Jersey, point out that the community as a whole has a responsibility for the retarded. There can be no satisfactory program for aiding them, according to him, without the co-operation of many groups and agencies. This certainly includes the church.

For purposes of religious education the retarded can be roughly divided into three groups: (1) First, there are those who are educable. They attend public schools, either in regular classes or in special classes. Though they are retarded, they can profit somewhat from a regular program of religious education. (2) Second are those whose retardation is such that they cannot benefit from a regular program. They are in the community but cannot participate in regular educational programs, either public or religious. (3) Third are those who are so severely retarded that they are in institutions.

Most churches do not have enough mentally retarded children to form a special class for them. If the child can participate at all with other children, it is well for him to do so. However, this does present problems. In an institution the religious education services are geared to meet the special needs of the children. In a regular church school class this cannot be done. The retarded child often cannot read the church school material. He cannot understand the same vocabulary as other children. He finds it difficult to take part in class discussions. It is difficult for him to comprehend the lesson. Aside from the job of teaching so that all children understand the lesson, the teacher has the task of helping the class to understand and accept the child as one of the group, of helping him to feel he belongs to, and can contribute to, the group in some way. This takes great skill and great understanding on the part of the teacher.

The retarded child who cannot be integrated into the regular program is a much more difficult problem. He needs more supervision and more care. Some need almost constant supervision. The quarterlies and church school papers developed for the average child do not fit the needs of the severely mentally handicapped child. For these reasons it would be well if churches, either individually or collectively, would provide special classes for such children as the public schools do.

There have been a few such efforts. In 1952 the Evanston Council of Churches, Evanston, Illinois, sponsored an interdenominational church school for retarded children. The purpose of the school was threefold:

(1) to give retarded children (trainable children) who are unable to take part in regular church school classes a special class they may attend Sunday morning at a church while their parents attend church services;

(2) to enable parents to go to the church of their choice;

(3) to give parents the assurance of the interest and concern of the church for them and their children.[2]

Archie Oliver, a trained and experienced teacher of the mentally handicapped in the public school, was secured as the director, with two assistants, a trained nursery school teacher, and student teachers to help. Fifteen children were registered; the average attendance was seven.

The First Lutheran Church of Long Beach, California, conducted a Summer Bible School for retarded children. Fifteen were registered. They came from all parts of the city and their ages ranged from nine years to twenty-two. They were children who had been unable to attend regular church school programs, so most of them had not had any religious instruction.[3]

The Christ Lutheran Church of St. Paul, Minnesota, operates a Sunday school for retarded children during the church service. In this way the parents can attend the worship service while the children receive their religious training. They are divided into four groups: boys who can't read, girls who can't read, boys who can read, and girls who can read. Older children who can't read are placed in the reading group because of their age and size.[4]

These are isolated instances but are indications of some

2 Mimeographed statement of the "Church School Class for Retarded Children," Evanston Council of Churches, Department of Christian Education, Evanston, Illinois.

3 Mimeographed pamphlet, "Sunday School for Mentally Retarded Children."

4 Reported in the Bulletin of the Good Shepherd Lutheran Home, August, 1954, p. 4.

efforts that are being made and are suggestive of the type of thing that might be done. If special programs are attempted, they should be carried out carefully so that no stigma is attached and so that retarded children and their families do not get their hopes built up for something that will be helpful, only to have it dropped because of lack of preparation and planning.

General Principles

There are certain general principles that apply to the teaching of all retarded children whether in a regular class with other children or in a special class. It must be recognized that their attention span is short; about ten minutes is all they can sustain attention without some change or break. Long speeches, lectures, presentations of any sort will lose their attention and their interest. Because their comprehension is much slower, they need to have things repeated often. A liberal amount of drill and repetition must be included. What would be monotonous repetition for the gifted child is a necessity for the retarded child.

He must develop at his own rate of speed. He cannot be hurried. To attempt to "crowd" him to keep up with others only leads to confusion, frustration, and opens the way for discipline problems.

These children have particular difficulty in understanding abstract generalizations. For this reason teachings on character and religion must be specific and simple. The retarded child must be taught right from wrong, but it takes a longer time for him to grasp and understand socially acceptable behavior.

Perhaps his greatest handicap is in the area of language. It is suggested that a good procedure for anyone who is dealing with retarded children is to stand aside and listen to a group in conversation and note the simplicity of the words they use. There is a strong tendency to assume that they understand the meaning of many words that are almost completely unintelligible to them. Anyone who has given an examination that includes very much verbalization to some of these children knows how many misconceptions they sometimes have. Such passages as the Lord's Prayer cannot be used meaningfully without interpretation of all of the words and phrases. Whether it is teaching, leading in worship, or personal counseling, the vocabulary must be kept very simple.

Since religion is filled with abstractions, ideas, and ideals, these should always, if possible, be clarified by illustrations and examples. Even then the moral should be explained and spelled out. For this reason visual aids have been very helpful in the work with the mentally handicapped. Slides, filmstrips, films, flannelgraphs do much to clarify the lesson and also to sustain and hold interest and attention.

As much as possible, the retarded child needs individualized instruction. For this reason classes for the retarded, or in which retarded are present, ideally should be small. This enables the teacher to adapt the teaching to the level of understanding of the child, to make explanations and to answer questions. It is good for him to be in a group, but he cannot profit from group teaching as his more gifted classmates can.

There is more to a class for retarded children than mere instruction. There is more value to participation in a class than can be measured by the knowledge that is gained. The teacher has more to contribute to the life of the retarded child than the imparting of information.

One of the major problems of the retarded child in the classroom is his attitude toward himself. Because of previous experiences of rejection or overprotection he often is completely lacking in self-confidence and self-esteem. The teacher must be conscious of these feelings and not contribute to them by assigning him tasks and responsibilities beyond his limitations that only contribute to his embarrassment and discouragement. Retarded children like other children like to take part in activities, but it must be on their own level. They need much encouragement, praise, and reward—never ridicule or scolding. Wherever possible, good work and behavior should be recognized and rewarded.

Each child needs to be recognized as an individual; he needs to feel that he "belongs" in the group, that he is accepted by the teacher and by the other children. This not only leads to better learning but does much to help the child come to an acceptance of himself and find satisfaction quite apart from the classroom.

This is one of the ways the church can serve as one of a community team that helps the retarded. A fellowship in which the retarded child or young person can participate in some activities provides a great service to him. This is especially important as a service to those older young people who may return to the community from a state or private school. The church can almost do more than any other agency in helping them become a part of a group within the community.

The church can do much to help the retarded if they can provide the opportunity for them to render a service. Though the task may be as simple as passing out hymnbooks or cleaning a blackboard, it gives the person a sense of worth. The retarded are used to receiving; they must be taught to give. The retarded too have a contribution to make. The church should help them make it, help them realize they have a part to play. For this reason the offering is important, quite apart from what they give. It is a means whereby they can share. Some have become very useful members of their church and community, generous with their time and their means.

The church should be careful that it does not add to the problems of the retarded. To be rejected by others in a church group is almost harder than in any other place. Consider the plight of the retarded youth who sits in a youth meeting and the speaker says that anyone can succeed if he will only work hard enough. This is true for the gifted child, but the retarded cannot succeed, no matter how hard he tries. The whole question of the recruitment for the ministry can create a problem. Because of the great shortage of ministers it is often stressed that all young people ought to consider the possibility of service in one of the full-time church vocations. The retarded person, too, has an interest in the church; he, too, would like to serve, but the possibility of four years of college work and three years of seminary are out of the question for him. He should not be led to feel that he is any less worthy, or that his service is less acceptable than that of others.

All of this emphasizes the importance of the teacher. One of the most significant things about the teacher is her own attitude. To be an effective and helpful teacher of the retarded one must accept them emotionally. This is true of all children, but it is especially true of the retarded. Only when they are accepted in this way can they develop attitudes of trust and confidence that are so essential to good instruction and to wholesome personality development. Any attitudes of pity or feeling that the child does not have an inherent worth in his own right will be felt by the child in some subtle and unexplainable way. It must be an attitude that is based on respect, on genuine affection, in religious terms on the realization that these children, or this child is a "child of God."

The ideal teacher of religion with retarded children would be one who is trained in special education, one who has a knowledge of the psychology of the retarded, and one who is thoroughly trained in religion with a deep personal experience of the Christian faith. Such people are very rare indeed; in fact, the vast majority of churches carry on their programs of religious education with volunteer help. Even in those places where special classes could be set up, it is difficult to find someone with all of these qualifications and all of this training. This does not mean that the job cannot be done. Someone is needed who is genuinely interested in children, someone with great patience and understanding who believes in the worth of these children and who has a real religious faith and desires to help where she can. Much can be gained by visiting the public schools where they have special classes for the retarded and by reading some of the books and articles that have been prepared for public education.

The teacher of the retarded should work closely with the parents. In addition, of course, the parents must work with the teacher. Only as the teacher understands the home, the background in which the child lives, the attitudes of the parents, and so forth, can she understand the child. This is not only a help to the child but is often a great help and service to the parents. Only when the parents and teacher can work together can the maximum value be achieved for the child.

Religious Education in Institutions for the Retarded

The religious education of the retarded differs from the religious education of the gifted in that there is one group that is separated, its members are together in institutions, either public or private. The pastor and the church have an interest in such institutions for a variety of reasons. Some of the children of families in his congregation may be sent to such institutions. The pastor has a real service to render to the child and to the family when this takes place. When an institution for the retarded is located in the vicinity of the church, there is often an opportunity and at times a responsibility to provide a direct service on a volunteer or part-time basis to the children there. Some pastors will want to become full-time chaplains of institutions for the retarded. Everyone, as a public-minded citizens, is interested in the welfare of the people in all of our institutions, whatever they may be.

In institutions for the retarded there are three general groups or types that might be mentioned for our purposes here: (1) There is the group of those who are so severely retarded that they cannot be reached for any training, spiritual or otherwise. They are custodial cases at the very lowest IQ range. (2) There are those in the slightly higher range who will probably always remain in the institution. They can be trained to perform some useful tasks within the institution but cannot be expected to maintain themselves in society. (3) There are those who, after training, may be returned to their homes and communities.

Little in the way of a religious program can be planned

for the first group. They cannot understand words; they cannot grasp ideas; they cannot utilize curriculum materials. They do have feelings. They can respond to a relationship of affection in their own way and at the level of their own understanding. The spirit of Christian compassion should be extended to all. The other two groups can enjoy and profit from religious training.

Another factor that must be taken into account is the number of physically handicapped present in such institutions. The percentage is much higher than among the average population. Some are spastic; some are emotionally disturbed as well as intellectually retarded. Many have not had the physical and medical care that they needed. Some are homeless; some are born out of wedlock; all types and descriptions are found in institutions for the retarded. Some have been in an institution for retarded children for many years and consequently are older than most of the others.

What has been done in the past to provide religious training and, to a large extent, what is being done in the present is dependent upon volunteer services of those who are in the community in which the institution is located. Although this has obvious weaknesses and limitations, there are also distinct benefits: in the first place, it makes available religious training where it did not otherwise exist and, in the second place, it takes the life of the church, a part of the outside world, into the life of the institution.

Not everyone is qualified for such work. The Training School of Kentucky, which makes much use of volunteer groups and leadership, has prepared a handbook, written by Chaplain Leonard Morgan, Jr. It points out that everyone gets disturbed at times in working with such children but, in the main,

groups of volunteers who come into an institution for the mentally defective should be made up of people who are

—temperamentally and emotionally fitted to work with men, women, boys and girls who are mentally deficient and mentally, physically and spiritually ill,

—willing to accept the responsibility of working as part of a hospital team whose purpose is to help handicapped individuals,

—organized within themselves in such a way that they can as a group work efficiently together,

—willing to give a certain specified amount of their time to help in a planned program of therapy for patients,

—capable of leading people in games, etc.[5]

The workers should have some understanding of the nature of mental deficiency and the things that can be expected of the retarded. The teacher should know the techniques of the lower grades; in fact, some will work at the kindergarten and preacademic level. All of the principles mentioned earlier apply here, and more so. The workers with the retarded must keep in mind that they are talking to people with the mentality of children and that simplicity must be the first requirement.

The curriculum for the average Sunday church school does not apply in the institutional setting. During the war a Civilian Public Service unit was assigned to the Pennhurst State School in Pennsylvania. They carried on a project of religious education that was directed by Howard Schomer, a Congregational minister. This project was

[5] Mimeographed pamphlet, Morgan, "Volunteer Groups for the Mental Defective," Kentucky Training Home.

studied by a joint committee of the National Council of
Churches and what was then the International Council of
Religious Education. They found that some materials prepared for regular church schools could be used, but much
of it did not fit.

> Especially among the boys we sensed that the stories were too
> sweet, too remote from their own often embittering experience
> of life on the streets, in chaotic homes, and now in . . . the
> atmosphere of the institution. The second defect of the lessons
> for our groups was their social illustrations and assumptions.
> Mothers, fathers, grandparents, sisters and brothers, homes,
> personal bed-rooms, churches, stores, trips—all the characters
> and scenes in the drama of daily life for the normal children
> were only part of blurred and mixed memories for most of our
> segregated and often abandoned children.[6]

While the problems of volunteers in an institution are
many, and while the results may seem very small, the re-
wards can be significant and the values that come from
such efforts may be vastly greater than appears on the sur-
face. As the handbook mentioned above states, ". . . to the
volunteer the time spent with a patient may seem very
small. To the patient the visit can be a very wonderful
experience."[7]

The best solution is to have a full-time resident chaplain
within the institution who can direct all religious activities.
He can fulfill the traditional functions of the minister, conducting public worship and classes of religious training,
and he can direct the program of volunteers who, even as
in a local church, help with a church school. He has the
further advantage that he can supplement the program of
religious instruction with personal counseling and can be

---

6 Schomer, "Religious Ministry to the Mentally Deficient," Reprint from *American
Journal of Mental Deficiency*, July 1946, pp. 77-78.
7 *Ibid.*, p. 4.

of tremendous help to the parents of the children under his care.

Chaplain Leonard Morgan, of the Kentucky Training Home, says that there are three groups that respond best to counseling by the chaplain. They are the new patients, the very young patients, and the patients who never had a healthy relationship with any parent or 'parent substitute. With such children the chaplain can do much to help create a better adjustment between the patient and the institution, in aiding the patient to accept his limited ability and alleviate certain behavior problems.[8]

Some of the problems of retarded children may seem small and perhaps childish, but to them they are real and should be handled with understanding and care. Some of these problems are religious in nature. Chaplain Melvin Oehrtman, of the Columbus State School, Columbus, Ohio, says many of them

have either had or recently formulated strange and unusual concepts about God. He is often pictured as immature, primitive, partial and unstable adult, One whose favor must be courted, or One who must be fooled into granting desired favors. Of course, this is not a picture of God which is held exclusively by residents of a state school. Yet a more healthy attitude can be substituted for the many misconceptions that are held.[9]

He said the most frequent problem which was presented to the chaplain was one of parental rejection.

Probation and Commitment to the institution most often are experiences that are not forgotten. Often a picture of complete parental and family rejection is formulated by the child.

[8] Morgan, "The Chaplain and the Mental Defective," Reprint from American Journal of Mental Deficiency, July 1953.
[9] Oehrtman, "Chaplaincy Service for the Mentally Retarded," National Association for Retarded Children.

The child often feels that God, too, has rejected him. It is precisely at this point that very effective work can be done by the chaplain. To help the newly admitted realize that someone is interested in him, that God has not forsaken him, that the attendants and matrons are new-found friends is a most important function of the chaplain.[10]

One of the most helpful functions is to work with the parent. He can do much to help the child accept the situation, relieve his anxieties about the institution, free him from a sense of guilt. Often they feel more at ease in discussing some of these matters with the chaplain than with any other representative of the institution. The very knowledge that a chaplain is there gives them much reassurance.

The chaplain works in an interdenominational setting. In state institutions every variety of religious background is represented. Participation in religious activities is voluntary and dependent primarily upon the wishes of the parents. The difference in denominations is incomprehensible to the child and the major emphases are on those beliefs that are common to all groups.

The chaplaincy in institutions for the retarded is still in its infancy. Very few studies have been made of the work and only a few articles have appeared, such as those we have quoted here. Most of these have appeared in the *American Journal for Mental Deficiency,* with the exception of one or two in the *International Journal of Religious Education.*

The little that has been done indicates that retarded children are receptive to religious teaching; they seem to enjoy participation in religious activities, provided the activities are relatively simple and the children have been prepared as to what to expect and how to behave. Officials

10 *Ibid.,* p. 256.

and workers in institutions for the retarded say that they can notice a difference in the behavior of those receiving such instruction and guidance. Many institutions have no provisions for a religious program. They, too, have problems of budget, finance, facilities, and personnel. Rather than being critical of their work, we should make efforts to provide such services. There has been a trend toward a change in philosophy of such institutions from custodial care to training and rehabilitation so that the children can return to the community and live lives of normal usefulness. Along with educational and vocational training should go moral and spiritual training so that they can become parts of the community, participants in the church but, most important of all, that they may have the values that come from religious faith and acceptance.

Chapter X

Helping Retarded Youth: The Guidance of the Retarded

Any discussion of counseling with the retarded should begin with the affirmation that favorable results are possible. Some people who would be quite enthusiastic about the possibilities of improving behavior with average or superior children would feel that similar efforts with retarded children would have little value. It is true that the counselor with the retarded must realize that he is working with a person of limited ability; results are not as dramatic; more time, more patience and more skill are required to produce results but the possibilities are there.[1] As an article in the *American Journal of Mental Deficiency* states, "Much of the social and economic ineffectiveness of the mentally retarded is so tragically unnecessary. Adequate counseling can serve to increase his effectiveness in all areas of his activities so that he may become self-supporting and an asset to society."[2]

The goals of counseling with the retarded will be simpler and more modest than they would be with more intelligent youth. As the Pollocks say in their book, "The mentally

[1] Since the completion of this manuscript there has been published a very excellent book edited by Charles L. Stacey and Manfred L. De Martino, *Counseling and Psychotherapy with the Mentally Retarded*, The Free Press, 1957. Had it appeared earlier, it undoubtedly would have been quoted in these pages.

[2] Lloyd N. Yepsen, "Counseling the Mentally Retarded," in *American Journal of Mental Deficiency*, Oct. 1952, p. 206.

retarded will never find a place in the Hall of Fame, nor will they ever become leaders in the community."[3] Nevertheless they can become good followers; they do have a contribution to make; they do have feelings and problems that need to be solved. Furthermore, without proper guidance they can fall prey to influences which can result not only in misfortune for them but which make them problems to society. In fact, some people feel that the duller the child the more he needs individual help.

As in all counseling, the attitudes of the counselor are most important. More important than the techniques he uses is the rapport that he is able to establish with the counselee. As in all counseling, if a person wishes to be effective with the retarded, he must make an honest effort to understand them; he must be able to see the situation from their perspective, but, most important of all, he must genuinely like them; he must have the inner conviction that they are worth while, that their problems, their feelings, their needs are important, that they are significant in the eyes of God.

The principles and methods of counseling the retarded are similar to those used in counseling anyone else, but there is likely to be a different emphasis. The nondirective, or client-centered, approach does not apply here as it does with the gifted. The basic philosophy and purposes of counseling are essentially the same. The young person is accepted, with all of his feelings and limitations. He is permitted to talk and release his tensions. But he cannot be expected to enter into the relationship in the same manner as does the gifted child. He is not as capable of self-direction. He does not have the knowledge and cannot gain the

3 See Pollock and Pollock, New Hope for the Retarded, Sargent 1953, p. 13.

insight for making decisions as the gifted can. There are occasions when more directive guidance seems necessary. This is especially true in such matters as educational and vocational choices, where the young person may have ambitions and desires but is not aware of the requirements of these choices or of his own limitations. The counselor must be careful that he guides and does not dictate, and the young person must be as free as possible to make his own choices and decisions, always in the light of his background and limitations. In other words, one must be somewhat eclectic in counseling with the retarded, adapting his methods to the needs of the individual and to the demands of the situation. Lloyd N. Yepsen points out that sometimes the counseling is supportive; sometimes it consists in the giving of sound advice; sometimes it may be a constructive emotional appeal to guide the behavior of the retarded person in a desirable course of action; sometimes it is the skillful use of suggestion or motivation; sometimes it is stimulating and checking understanding; sometimes it is helping him gain insight. Of course, in actual practice it is never one or the other of the above functions but a combination of all of them. The important thing that he emphasized is that behavior is modifiable. This is true of the retarded as it is of others and therefore they can respond to counseling. Many retarded people have not reached their full potential because they have not been understood and have not had the benefit of adequate counseling and guidance.[4]

The retarded person is highly subject to suggestion; in fact, this is one of his weaknesses. The counselor should be aware of this and be cautious in what he says and does. The

---

[4] Yepsen, *op. cit.*

retarded youth may indicate that he understands a situation just to please the counselor when actually he does not. Nothing can be taken for granted. One must always explain the obvious. As in the religious education of the retarded, the vocabulary must be kept very simple. He cannot work on a plan that extends too far into the future. He must deal with situations that are here and now. For this reason some retarded people need constant guidance and direction.

The problems of the retarded are as varied as are the problems of average people. Some of them have religious problems; some of them need religious guidance. This is especially true of those young people who come to the age of church membership. Their more gifted classmates are entering classes for church membership and they wish to also. The pastor could well give extra time and attention to these young people who cannot comprehend as quickly or as deeply. They may be making this decision simply because others in their class are, or because their parents are urging them to do so, without any understanding of what its meaning should be. Retarded young people can at times develop a real feeling of God's acceptance, as much as the average young person.

The retarded young person needs an understanding of his own limitations. Sometimes this comes quite easily. Many youngsters are not at all disturbed by the fact that they are in the third grade when all others their age have been advanced to the fifth. Others get a very unrealistic view of their possibilities and consider goals and objectives that are beyond their attainment. This is often accentuated by parents who have had unrealistically high goals for their children academically and vocationally. Many of these disappointments and heartaches could be avoided with the proper counseling and guidance in childhood.

Although we are talking primarily about retarded children and young people, we must remember that there are also mentally retarded adults in the community. They are entitled to the same consideration and understanding as others. While they are mature physically and chronologically, they have the mentality of children. Some are discharged or paroled from training schools or institutions. This is almost always a difficult transition. The pastor and the church can do much to help them feel accepted in the community and have friends in whom they can trust and confide.

One of their major problems is a vocational one. Ours is a culture in which one's position and prestige are determined largely by his vocation. This is where the feeling of the family may be most acute. The retarded person may come to his pastor or youth leader with his vocational problem. Vocational guidance is a long and highly complicated process. It is not completed in one interview. It involves an evaluation of a person's abilities; it requires a knowledge of the world of work, the requirements of each occupation, and the opportunities that are available.

The minister has an important part to play. He can meet the person with understanding. He can help him think through his possibilities. He must also recognize his own limitations of training and experience. He should not attempt to do what others can do better. One of his chief functions is to help the person get to those agencies that can give him specialized help.

Since 1943 the mentally handicapped have been eligible for special guidance and training through the program of vocational rehabilitation sponsored jointly by the state and federal governments. They are prepared to assist those young people who are of working age, those who have passed certain medical and psychological examinations and are thus eligible for such help and are able to profit from such training. Their experience has proved that many mentally retarded persons, previously doomed to idleness and uselessness, can be trained to become well-adjusted citizens who are able to carry on some means of employment. It is estimated that 70 per cent of those with an IQ between 50 and 70 are capable of earning their own living.

Usually the work that they can do is routine work; that is, it is under supervision and requires little education. Several studies have been made as to where such people find employment. Boys are usually placed in mills or factories doing unskilled labor; some are on farms; some do simple mechanical work; some are in the personal service fields. Girls find employment in factories, laundries, homes, and restaurants. The Pollocks list positions their graduates have filled: a helper in a building wrecking crew, a shipper in a mattress factory, a bus boy in a hotel, a packager in a tea company, an owner of an ice cream truck, a packer in a cookie factory, an errand boy for a jewelry firm, and so forth. These jobs need to be done and these young people need to be taught the sacredness of all honest effort. Wise guidance, friendly encouragement, together with opportunities for training, may help some young person with limited ability to go much farther than he otherwise would have gone; he might even surpass some people of greater ability who did not have the guidance and encouragement.

Some of these people cannot earn their own living, but they can be partially self-supporting, either in part-time employment or in sheltered workshops. This is good for them even if they earn only spending money.

One of their problems is that they are forced to compete with people of average or normal ability. It is true that most of their work is of the unskilled variety, but 20 per cent of all the nation's work falls in this class. Many people of average ability must do unskilled work. Because of compulsory school laws they have to stay in school until they are sixteen. Here they are treated as "slow learners," and are given individual help and attention. Many schools follow the pattern of automatic promotion, creating the illusion they are progressing at the same rate as their classmates; then they are thrust into the economic world where their disabilities are neither known nor recognized and are forced to shift for themselves in a highly competitive environment designed for adults without limitations of ability.

Sometimes the church shares in the creation of this problem. Because of the very real shortage of ministers, extensive programs of recruitment are taking place. Oftentimes these emphases are directed to large groups of young people. In one mass meeting of several hundred young people an appeal was made for all young people to consider the needs of the church. Those who were willing were asked to commit themselves that night to the ministry or the mission field. Several responded, among them a retarded boy who had not been able to finish high school. It was a great experience for him; here was something he thought he could do. Later he went to his pastor to find out how he could become a preacher. When he learned it required four years of college and three years of graduate training, he was very much surprised.

At a youth conference in one of our Midwestern states a rather strong appeal was made for full-time life recruits. An impressive and highly emotional consecration service was planned. All the young people were standing in a circle when the appeal was made for those who would give themselves to full-time Christian service. They were asked to step forward and many of them did. One was a mentally retarded boy.

This does not mean that these young people cannot render some Christian service. It does mean that it will probably not be in the ministry. While intelligence alone is not the criterion for determining who should study for the ministry, the chances of completing four years of college and three years of seminary are pretty remote for the person who does not have an IQ of 100 or better. It leaves the pastor with a difficult situation. These young people were challenged and inspired. If he discourages them at such a time, he adds to a long list of disappointments. If he doesn't, he puts them in a position to be let down later.

Whatever the vocation that is selected, certain principles should be kept in mind.

1. The job must be within the individual's intellectual ability. Any attempt to fill a position beyond his capacity only leads to disappointment.

2. Ability is not the only factor that must be considered. A study conducted by the office of vocational rehabilitation revealed that their counselors dealt with personality problems as much as they did with vocational ones. The retarded need help in establishing work habits, in the ability to get along with their fellow workers, in their punctuality, reliability, and so forth.

3. It is important that they be located with those who

understand the situation, that they have a boss or employer who will not exploit them. The community itself can cause a problem. The files of a rehabilitation office tell of a young man with an IQ of 54. He was placed in a job as a car-washer and was doing very well. The employer had been prepared for the project and was quite understanding about it but he was not aware of the problems created by the other employees. They misplaced his sponge; they hid his hat; they turned off the water while he was working, then mysteriously turned it on when he didn't expect it. They called him "the dummy." Through it all he was hurt, angry, and confused. The result was that he quit and an attempt at rehabilitation that could have worked out very well was destroyed.

4. The work selected should not be work that endangers others or that requires too much responsibility. The person must be motivated or he will not stick to a job. He needs to see that his work is important. He must be taught that all honest work is important. He needs recognition and encouragement. If he is doing his best, he deserves just as much credit as a more brilliant person who is accomplishing greater things but who may not be using his capacities to any greater extent. After all, the man with two talents received the same reward as the man with five because he had been faithful with that which had been entrusted to him.

5. When possible, the work should not be seasonable but year-round.

6. It is well that parents be included in any plans of vocational guidance. We shall speak more of that in the next section but the attitudes of parents can do much to assist or hinder the work of a counselor.

Anyone working with the retarded should know the resources to which he can turn for help. At times it may be a medical problem requiring a physician; at other times a psychological one requiring a psychologist or a psychiatrist; at other times it may be a family or social problem requiring a social worker. There are times when a speech therapist is needed, or when a youngster may get into difficulty or delinquency and may need an attorney. We have already referred to special education in the public schools and to the office of vocational rehabilitation. One counselor in the field of vocational rehabilitation said that when the referral came from a minister there was usually better family assistance and often the backing of church groups that resulted in more "staying power" on the part of the client.[5] One of the pastor's greatest services can be to get the retarded people to those individuals and agencies that have training, skill, and resources that he does not have. The retarded and even their families often do not know what services are available or how to make contact with them. This does not mean that the pastor separates himself from them. He still maintains his position as a pastor. He still "stands by" in time of need, which is one of his greatest contributions. One of the problems of the retarded is that he is seen by many specialists, each from one particular point of view and in terms of one particular service. The pastor should see him as a whole in the light of all his needs and all his experience and all his possibilities.

The Pastor and the Parents of the Retarded Child

In helping a retarded child, one of the greatest services the pastor can render is to help the parents of the child.

[5] Cf. *American Journal of Mental Deficiency.* Oct., 1952, p. 313.

This has a double value, for the parents, too, have a problem. "No child stands alone." The retarded child is a part of a family. What happens to the family affects the child and, of course, the opposite is also true.

Ministry to the parents of the retarded is quite different from a ministry to the parents of the gifted. It may come almost from the day of the birth of the child. Some forms of mental retardation can be recognized at once. When a doctor finds it necessary to inform a couple that this is the case, it is always a discouraging, bewildering, and almost overwhelming experience. They need the help of everyone possible at such a time, especially of the pastor. He should be there to help them face the situation, to make the necessary adjustment, and to give them the feeling that there is someone standing by who understands.

Recognition of the fact that a child is retarded may come later, after the child is a bit older; perhaps even after some unpleasant experiences at school. Though the family may have suspected that something is wrong and long have had questions in their minds, still, when the physician or psychologist makes his diagnosis, it comes as something of a shock. At this time they need the presence of a pastor.

In many cases the family turns to the pastor, seeking his help at such a time. A superintendent of a large state training school for the retarded said, "After the physician has been consulted about a retarded child, the next person to hear about it is usually the pastor."[6] For this reason the pastor should know something about the problem he is asked to face. He should know the role he is best qualified to play and the resources to which the family can turn. He should encourage the people to secure the best medical and

[6] In a letter from Dr. Arthur Westwell, President American Association for Mental Deficiency.

psychological advice that is available. It is not his place to make a diagnosis. He should guard against giving easy or false reassurance. "I'm sure your child will be all right" or "He'll probably outgrow it" are unfair and even cruel statements if they are not true. This is for a specialist to say. The pastor can do much to relieve anxiety, a sense of shame, a needless sense of guilt, and can give the reassurance that comes from the fact that he is standing by. He shares this experience with them.

It is important when the parents are told of such a condition that they have full and accurate information. They should have all their questions answered insofar as this is possible. Their problems should be faced fully and frankly. Since oftentimes this is not done, the parents may bring many of their questions to the pastor. Again he should not attempt to take the place of the specialist, but he should know the basic principles about mental retardation and he should know where the answers can be found. Through it all he should maintain the attitude and position that he is searching, along with the parents, for the right answers.

Families react differently to such a situation. Some families may accept it emotionally and intellectually; others may find it extremely difficult. There are certain patterns that are quite common. There is almost always an element of shock, of surprise, almost of horror and of grief. There is an element of uncertainty, for it usually means a change of plans; it means giving up many of the hopes and dreams they have held in anticipation. There is a certain amount of embarrassment and often a sense of guilt. Let one parent describe his family's feelings:

A thousand thoughts raced across my brain with kaleidoscopic rapidity. Was this the result of heredity? Was there no hope at all? Why did this have to happen to me? Why had God singled me out from all other men, to place this burden upon me? Why? Why? Why?

And then in the days that followed, the queer, hysterical thoughts that kept sweeping over me like an engulfing wave—the false sense of shame. What would people think? How could I face them? What would I say? What did the future hold? How could I go on living?

. . . what silent agonies, what repressed hopes, what buried miseries we expressed in those dreadful days.[7]

Fortunately this family worked out its problem to a good adjustment, but these statements express the feelings of many.

Some parents refuse to recognize the existence of the problem. They may refuse to accept the diagnosis of the experts. There may be a frantic and fruitless search for other doctors; they may even resort to quacks. They may blame the teachers for their failure to teach their child, or insist that he could do things if he were given the chance.

Very frequently parents are burdened with an unnecessary sense of guilt. They feel they must have sinned to have brought this about. They may feel resentment that they have been forced to deal with such a situation. Such resentment may be transferred to the child. They may tend to blame him for their embarrassment.

The pastor, because of his position, is the one best suited to deal with such questions as guilt. He can do as much as or more than anyone else to relieve such feelings and to bring a sense of comfort and reassurance. Dr. Jacob, superintendent of the Vineland School for the Retarded, says that about 40 per cent of their work is directed toward

7 "The Three Stages in the Growth of a Parent of a Mentally Retarded Child," Boyd, pamphlet, National Association for Retarded Children.

giving parents such comfort. He also states that the pastor is ideally suited for such a service.[8]

Sometimes a religious question is raised in people's minds. How can God permit this to happen? Have we sinned that this should be the result? It may cause people to question God himself. These are questions that a pastor must be prepared to face. Religion can also provide a great resource at such times. An educator, writing on the subject, says that parents of retarded children who have a religious outlook have an advantage over those who do not. They can "be helped to understand that every human being is equal in the sight of God and that all God's children are of infinite worth."[9] A medical journal reports a study of the parents of retarded children in 85 families. Investigators sought to find out what parents' attitudes were and what things were of greatest help to them. More than 25 per cent of the group spoke of the positive role played by religion.[10] The conclusion was that there needs to be a closer collaboration between the clergyman, the physician, the psychologist, and others working with the retarded. The pastor needs to take the lead in such a relationship, by showing his willingness to help, his willingness to become a part of a co-operative team that serves both the child and his family.

Parents need information about the retarded child, what he can do and what he cannot do, what can rightfully be expected of him and what ought not be expected of him. They also need counseling regarding their own feelings. The focus of the pediatrician, the psychologist, the special-

8 From a personal letter.

9 Laycock, "Helping Parents Accept Exceptional Children," in *Journal for Exceptional Children*, February, 1952, reprint.

10 Reported in Zwerling, "Initial Counseling of Parents with Mentally Retarded Children," Reprint from *Journal of Pediatrics*, April, 1954.

ist, whoever he may be, is usually on the child, as of necessity it must be. There is no one to give full consideration to the parents, their happiness, their feeling of shame, their uncertainty, unless the pastor does.

All of the experts agree that "parents must accept the child emotionally." That is such a common statement that we expect it to appear somewhere in every article or book on the subject. This is true of all children, whether they are retarded or not, but it is much more difficult with the retarded. His need for such acceptance is just as great if not greater. He needs to feel that he is loved, that he belongs. Let us quote one authority. "Parents of an exceptional child can help him effectively only by accepting him as he is, without embarrassment, resentment, shame, guilt or resignation."[11] This is true, but it is easier said than done. If parents are to be expected to do it, they may need help. The help they need is not simply telling them they "ought" to do it; that may only increase their feelings of inadequacy and failure. They should be permitted to "talk out" their problem, to express their feelings, to release what has been called the "intense repressed forces."[12]

Very few parents can be completely objective about a retarded child. They need someone who understands, someone with whom they can express their feelings, someone to help them with their plans, someone who can help them understand and accept the reality of the situation.

Parents need to be helped to see the child as he really is, not as they would like him to be. Because parents oftentimes do not have a realistic understanding of the child's limitations a strained relationship may develop between

11 Laycock, op. cit., p. 3.
12 Cf. Journal of Clinical Psychology, April, 1953, article by Weingold and Harmuth, "Group Guidance for Parents of Mentally Retarded Children," p. 20.

parent and child. A recognition of the fact that a child is retarded may lead to an attitude of pity or overprotection. There may be an overcompensation for their own feelings of humiliation to cover up their unconscious rejection of the child. Whereas some parents, not realizing the limitations, may demand too much of the child, others may not demand enough. They may surround him with too much sympathy, too much protection.

Parents must realize that little things are important. The retarded child must feel that he is a part of the group, a part of the family. If he can share in family activities and responsibilities around the home, even in a minor way, he is helped. Any complaining about his presence or the extra work it entails is harmful, as it would be to a normal child as well.

The parents of mentally retarded children have many questions they need to discuss with someone. They need factual information in order to make plans. The parents of mentally retarded children will come to recognize that goals and plans for a retarded child must of necessity be different from those for a normal or gifted child. Educational and vocational objectives cannot be the same. As a result, they have questions about schools, about vocational opportunities, about the possibilities of marriage. One of the big questions is how the child will survive economically. These questions become increasingly pertinent as the child grows older. They also can lead to a more strained relationship with the family as the child comes to the age when other children are moving on to college or are entering the vocational field, and he remains dependent upon the family.

This is not only a matter of expense but one of prestige.

It has been demonstrated that retarded young people can be trained to do some jobs. Many times parents cannot accept emotionally the kind of job which a retarded young person can do. For this reason it is important that vocational guidance of retarded youth include the parents. Workers in such areas as vocational rehabilitation and special education sometimes find that parents nullify all their efforts when they do not recognize that what the young person does must be in terms of his abilities and they refuse to accept what he can be trained to do. If they can accept it, they give great reassurance to the young person and are of great assistance to the school or vocational counselor. The pastor should keep before both parents and youth the truth that all honest work is sacred in the sight of God.

One of the major difficulties is the attitudes of the community. Parents of the retarded are in a difficult situation in the community. People do have many unfortunate ideas about the retarded. The community has a mixture of attitudes including suspicion, pity, fear, and ridicule. Other parents wonder if their children should play with a retarded child. They may change their attitude toward his parents or may avoid them altogether. All of this increases the problems of the parents and much of this feeling can be transferred to the child.

The parents feel embarrassed. They could explain a child's illness; they don't want to discuss the fact that he is retarded. They may think that their standing in the community is impaired, as indeed it may be, in the minds of some. They may withdraw from social contacts and refuse to have visitors in the home. Their sense of embarrassment and shame may cause them to drop out of the church and to feel they no longer can share in its activities. If they have not been active in a church, this may make them feel they cannot ever be.

These attitudes of the community cannot be ignored. Parents of a retarded child must live in a society in which such attitudes exist. The church must recognize the problem. It must lend its influence to creating community attitudes that are more understanding and Christian. The pastor himself, by his own attitudes, by his own understanding, by his own relationship with the family, can do much to relieve the parents.

It must be recognized that the whole family is affected by the presence of a retarded child. It may result in marital disputes, a tendency to blame one or the other of the marriage partners, or a disagreement as to what procedures to follow in training and discipline.

Other children in the home have a problem. They face embarrassment at school and on the playground. They may suffer from the taunting, stinging remarks of other children, who sometimes reflect the attitudes of adults. When they get older, they may not want to invite their friends into their home in which the presence of a retarded brother or sister may be an embarrassment to them. These children too need guidance so that they will understand the situation and so that they do not have any unfortunate personality developments as a result. The Pollocks feel that in many cases the minister is the one best qualified to explain to an average child the situation regarding a retarded child.[13]

All of the problems lead to the one most difficult decision that the parents of a retarded child are called upon to make.

13 Cf. Pollock and Pollock, *op. cit.*, p. 28.

"Should we place our child in a school or institution for the retarded?" Oftentimes the physician or psychologist making the diagnosis gives little help. He is very busy. He does not have time to listen to parents and hear all of their worries and questions. From the standpoint of the diagnosis, the situation is clear. As a result, he may say rather bluntly, "The best thing for you to do is to put your child in an institution where he can receive the proper care." We hasten to add that this is not fair to some physicians and psychologists. Some of them show infinite patience and understanding; in fact, we feel that the majority do. We are saying that such things can happen and when they do the pastor has a tremendous responsibility.

The parents may come to such a decision on their own, or they may suspect that it is necessary before they have ever counseled with any specialist about it and may come to the pastor for his advice. The pastor cannot make the decision for them. He should not try. He can urge them to get the best specialized help available. He can help them to think it through. He can stand by them, share with them in this difficult experience.

It is a difficult decision because no answer fits every case. Each child and each family is different. Even the theories seem to contradict each other. In some ways the home seems the best. There can be more love and affection, more personal attention in a home than in any institution. In other ways there are advantages to an institution that the home cannot provide. Specialized training is available. The child is freed from the embarrassment of the community. He competes with equals, not always with those who are superior.

Even experience differs. An article in a popular magazine, entitled, "We Kept Our Retarded Child at Home," tells how very well the situation worked out, how very happy the family seemed with the solution.[14] An article in another journal reports just the opposite experience. This family tried to work it out at home but found that an institution offered more advantages and the child himself was happier. How is the poor parent to know what to do?

Each situation must be seen as an individual case and approached on that basis, but certain general principles apply. The three basic questions are, (1) What is best for this individual child? (2) What is best for the family? (3) What is best for society?

Within these three questions are an infinite variety of other questions, no one of which may determine the answer but all of which have a bearing on the decision. We are thinking of such questions as these: Will the handicap improve? What are the potentials of learning basic skills, such as speech and reading? What are the possibilities of training? Will the child be accepted in the neighborhood? in the public school? What are the facilities in the community for special education? vocational training? recreation? Would the child be happier at home than he would be with other children of equal ability? How will it affect the total family situation? What effect will it have on other children? What will be the expense? What are the financial resources? Who will care for the child in the future? What is the institution itself like? What are the attitudes of the administration? of the employees? Does such institution-

14 Piccola, "We Kept Our Retarded Child at Home," *Coronet*, November, 1955.

alization need to be permanent? Could a child later return to his home and community?[15]

Fortunately a decision in this matter does not usually have to be made in a hurry. It is not like an operation that may need to be performed at once. Parents can take time to consider, to seek guidance, to investigate various possibilities; in fact, in some ways, it is better if the decision is reached gradually. In this way parents can come to accept the idea; they can be sure they have all the information that is necessary for the making of such a choice. Often parents are helped if they can visit the institution and meet the people who will be caring for their child before reaching a final decision. On occasion the pastor might go with them on such a visit. He could be a real source of support in such an experience.

Whenever possible, such a decision should be one that is agreed upon by both parents. It is a difficult experience and when they are of one accord, they can support each other in it. On the other hand, if they do not agree, it can form the basis for real family difficulty.

After all factors have been considered, if it is felt that it is best that a child be placed in a school or an institution, it still is a difficult experience for the parents. Though the institution may meet all of the requirements, there still is a hesitation about leaving the child in someone else's care. At this time they need a pastor to support them in their decision and stand by them in this experience. This is a place where the presence of a resident chaplain in the institution has a great value to the family. He can provide

15 Cf. Ecob, "Deciding What's Best for Your Retarded Child," N.Y. State Society for Mental Health, State Charities Aid Association, 1955 ; "Forgotten Children," National Association for Mental Health, p. 22ff ; Heiser, *Our Backward Children*, Norton, 1955, pp. 126-8.

much comfort and reassurance out of his contacts with other families who have faced similar decisions.

If it is deemed best that the child remain at home, then they need further help. Raising a normal child is not easy, but raising a retarded child has particular problems. The pastor is not a specialist in this field and cannot be, but he should know the resources that can help. Many times the parents are at a loss and do not know of the facilities of special education, vocational rehabilitation, and other agencies that are available. The pastor should know of these services and the people who direct them. He should know both what they can do and what they cannot do. Sometimes parents get their hopes built too high, only to face another disappointment when it is found that some agency cannot produce dramatic or radical changes. The unfortunate thing is that so many go without any help when experience has proven that some worth-while things can be done.

There are some very helpful books and pamphlets on the subject. These are published by such groups as The National Association for Retarded Children, The National Association for Mental Health, the United States Department of Health Education and Welfare, Columbia University, and others. Reading a book or a pamphlet will not solve all the problems but it can give a great deal of insight into the nature of the situation and can make some very practical suggestions. We have listed some of the printed resources in the bibliography at the close of this book.

There are some parents' groups that have had very significant success. These associations of parents of retarded children have been able to provide some things that no other group or individual could provide. It helps relieve the feeling of shame and disappointment if parents

can become part of a group who also have the same problems. They gain many practical suggestions as they share
their experiences with others who are faced with similar
situations. The address of the nearest parents' group can
be obtained from The National Association for Retarded
Children, Inc., 99 University Place, New York 3, New
York.

None of these resources takes the place of religion and
the Christian faith. No group can take the place of the
church group. No specialist can take the place of a pastor.
His responsibility continues to minister to all in the name
of Him who said, ". . . as you did it to one of the least of
these my brethren, you did it to me."

Bibliography

This bibliography is prepared with the hope that it will be of some practical use for those who seek further information on this subject. Some may be parents, or church school teachers, or pastors or religious educators who want a bit more knowledge on the gifted or retarded. It is hoped there will be some who will make it a subject of rather extensive study. The material presented in these pages is admittedly introductory. Many further studies need to be made.

We have included only material that deals directly with either the question of the gifted or the retarded. We have not attempted to include studies of religious education, pastoral counseling, general counseling, etc. For this reason, with the exception of a few articles, there is very little here about religion, the church, or the work of the pastor.

Some of the best material is in pamphlet form. These are usually brief but well written and summarize some of the latest findings. This is not at all meant to be an exhaustive bibliography. It simply includes some of the better material that exists to date. We hope it will be helpful.

I. THE GIFTED

A. *Books and Pamphlets*

American Association for Gifted Children. *The Gifted Child,* edited by Paul A. Witty. Boston: D. C. Heath & Co., 1951.

Baker, Harry Jay. *Introduction to Exceptional Children.* New York: Macmillan Co., 1947.

Carroll, Herbert Allen. *Genius in the Making.* New York: McGraw-Hill Book Co., 1940.

Cox, Catharine Morris. *The Early Mental Traits of Three*

Hundred Geniuses (Genetic Studies of Genius, Vol. 2) Stanford, Calif.: Stanford University Press, 1926.

Cruickshank, William M., Ed. *Psychology of Exceptional Children and Youth.* Englewood Cliffs, N. J.: Prentice-Hall, Inc., 1955.

Cutts, Norma Estelle, and Moseley, Nicholas. *Bright Children; a Guide for Parents.* New York: G. P. Putnam's Sons, 1953.

Educational Policies Commission of the National Education Association. *Education of the Gifted.* Washington: Natonal Education Association, 1950.

Garrison, Karl C. *Psychology of Exceptional Children.* New York: Ronald Press, 1950.

Hildreth, Gertrude H. and others. *Educating Gifted Children at Hunter College Elementary School.* New York: Harper & Brothers, 1952.

Passow, A. Harry, and others. *Planning for Talented Youth.* New York: Horace Mann-Lincoln Institute, Teachers College, Columbia University, 1955.

Scheifele, Marian. *The Gifted Child in the Regular Classroom.* New York: Teachers College, Columbia University, 1953.

Terman, Lewis M., and others. *The Gifted Child Grows Up* (Genetic Studies of Genius, Vol. 4) Stanford Calif.: Stanford University Press, 1947.

Witty, Paul Andrew. *Helping the Gifted Child.* Chicago: Science Research Associates, 1953.

Worcester, Dean Amory. *The Education of Children of Above-Average Mentality.* Lincoln: University of Nebraska Press, 1956.

B. *Periodical articles and bulletins*

Crawford, W. L., and others. "What Are We Doing for the Superior Child?" *Northwestern Reviewing Stand,* June 1952.

Gowan, John C. "The Underachieving Gifted Child, A Problem for Everyone," *Exceptional Children,* April 1955.

Havighurst, R. J., and others. "Are the Community and the School Failing the Unusual Child?" *University of Chicago Round Table,* April 1952.

Martens, Elise H. "Curriculum Adjustments for Gifted Children," *U.S. Office of Education Bulletin,* 1946, No. 1.

Strang, Ruth M. "Guidance of the Gifted," *Personnel and Guidance Journal,* October 1952.

Terman, Lewis M. "The Discovery and Encouragement of Exceptional Talent," *American Psychologist,* June 1954.

II. THE RETARDED

A. *Books and Pamphlets*

Baker, Harry Jay. *Introduction to Exceptional Children.* New York: Macmillan Co., 1947.

Boyd, Dan. *The Three Stages in the Growth of a Parent of a Mentally Retarded Child.* New York: National Association for Retarded Children, 1953.

Chamberlain, Naomi H., and Moss, Dorothy H. *The Three R's for the Retarded.* New York: National Association for Retarded Children, 1954.

Ecob, Katharine G. *The Retarded Child in the Community.* New York State Society for Mental Health, 1955.

Ecob, Katharine G. *Deciding What's Best for Your Retarded Child.* New York State Society for Mental Health, 1955.

Garrison, Karl C. *Psychology of Exceptional Children.* New York: Ronald Press, 1950.

Heiser, Karl F. *Our Backward Children.* New York: W. W. Norton & Co., 1956.

Jacob, Walter. *New Hope for the Retarded Child* (Public Affairs Pamphlet No. 210) New York, Public Affairs Committee, 1954.

Kirk, Samuel A., and Johnson, G. Orville. *Educating the Retarded Child*. Boston: Houghton Mifflin Co., 1951.

Kirk, Samuel A., and others. *You and Your Retarded Child*. New York: Macmillan Co., 1955.

Levinson, Abraham. *The Mentally Retarded Child; A Guide for Parents*. New York: John Day Co., 1952.

National Association for Mental Health. *Forgotten Children*. New York: National Association for Mental Health.

National Association for Mental Health. *If Your Child Is Slow*. New York: National Association for Mental Health.

National Association for Retarded Children. *The Child Nobody Knows*. New York: National Association for Retarded Children.

National Society for the Study of Education. *Education of Exceptional Children* (49th Yearbook, Part 2) Chicago: University of Chicago Press, 1950.

Pollock, Morris P. and Miriam. *New Hope for the Retarded*. Boston: Porter E. Sargent, Inc., 1953.

Sarason, Seymour Bernard. *Psychological Problems in Mental Deficiency*. New York: Harper & Brothers, 1953.

Smith, Marion F. *Teaching the Slow Learning Child*. New York: Harper & Brothers, 1954.

Stacey, Chalmers L., and DeMartino, Manfred F., Eds. *Counseling and Psychotherapy with the Mentally Retarded*. Chicago: Free Press, 1956.

Wallin, J. E. Wallace. *Education of Mentally Handicapped Children*. New York: Harper & Brothers, 1955.

World Health Organization. *The Mentally Subnormal Child*. New York: International Documents Service, 1954.

B. *Periodical articles and bulletins*

Cianci, Vincents. "The Problem of the Severely Retarded Child in Public Schools," *American Journal of Mental Deficiency*, April 1954.

Doll, Edgar A. "Counseling Parents of Severely Mentally Retarded Children," *Journal of Clinical Psychology,* April, 1953.

Drewry, Henry H. "Information for Parents of Mentally Retarded Children," *American Journal of Mental Deficiency,* January 1953.

Fields, Harold. "Who Makes the Best Teacher of Mentally Retarded Children?" *American Journal of Mental Deficiency,* October 1953.

Hill, M. E. "The Forward Look; The Severely Retarded Child Goes to School," *U. S. Office of Education Bulletin,* 1952, No. 11.

Johnson, George Orville, "Guidance for the Mentally Handicapped," *Journal of Exceptional Children,* January 1950.

Johnson, G. Orville, and Kirk, Samuel A. "Are Mentally-Handicapped Children Segregated in the Regular Grades?" *Journal of Exceptional Children,* December 1950.

Kanner, Leo. "Parents' Feelings About Retarded Children," *American Journal of Mental Deficiency,* January 1953.

Laycock, S. R. "Helping Parents To Accept Their Exceptional Children," *Exceptional Children,* February 1952.

Oliver, Archie S., Jr. "The Mentally Handicapped," *International Journal of Religious Education,* June 1954.

Piccola, Frank. "We Kept Our Retarded Child at Home," *Coronet,* November 1955.

Rautman, Arthur L. "The Seriously Retarded Child," *Mental Health,* 1946.

Schomer, Howard. "Religious Ministry to the Mentally Deficient," *American Journal of Mental Deficiency,* July 1946.

Stevenson, George S. "A Community Program for the Mentally Retarded," *American Jounrnal of Mental Deficiency,* April 1952.

Yepson, Lloyd N. "Counseling the Mentally Retarded," *American Journal of Mental Deficiency,* October 1952.

Yoder, H. W. "The Church and Retarded Children," *Children's Religion, February* 1957.

Zwerling, Israel. "Initial Counseling of Parents with Mentally Retarded Children," *Journal of Pediatrics,* April 1954.

"Counseling the Mentally Retarded and Their Parents," entire issue of *Journal of Clinical Psychology,* April 1953.

"Vocational Rehabilitation of the Mentally Retarded," entire issue of *American Journal of Mental Deficiency,* October 1952.

Index

187